ALONG THE
ROYAL ROADS TO
ANGKOR

ALONG THE ROYAL ROADS TO
ANGKOR

Photographs by
Hitoshi Tamura

Text by
Yoshiaki Ishizawa

New York WEATHERHILL Tokyo

Originally published in Japanese in 1999 as *Ankoru no Odo o Iku* by Tankosha Publishing Co., Ltd. Text © 1999 Yoshiaki Ishizawa. Photographs © 1999 Hitoshi Tamura.   © 1999 Tankosha Publishing Co., Ltd.

First English edition, 1999
Second Printing, 2001
Third Printing, 2003
Fourth Printing, 2004
Fifth Printing, 2005
Sixth Printing, 2006
Seventh Printing, 2007
Eighth Printing, 2008
Ninth Printing, 2010

Published in English by Weatherhill, Inc., New York and Tokyo. English edition protected by copyright under the terms of the International Copyright Union; all rights reserved. Printed in China.

Cataloging-in-Publication data available from the Library of Congress.

CONTENTS

ALONG THE ROYAL ROADS TO ANGKOR

Text and photographs by Hitoshi Tamura

ALL ROYAL ROADS LEAD TO ANGKOR

By Yoshiaki Ishizawa

Photographer's Afterword: Angkor's Long Silence
and a New Dawn

ALONG THE
ROYAL ROADS TO
ANGKOR

THE CITY OF THE GODS: ANGKOR WAT

Angkor Wat is a symbol of modern Cambodia, but also of the ancient Angkor Empire, with its vast network of roads weaving throughout all Indochina. Along those "royal roads," the kings of Angkor marched in brilliant royal processions; along those roads they also dispatched their armies of conquest. Angkor Wat, built in the early part of the twelfth century by the Angkor ruler Suryavarman II, is a Hindu temple. It was constructed as a royal tomb, and its

leading up to the third and innermost gallery is so steep as to be treacherous, and the design of the whole seems almost intended to rebuff the devotee. There are towers at each of the four corners of the innermost gallery, and the taller central sanctuary rises in their center, the peak of Mount Meru, the very center of the world. It was here, in this sacred space, that the secret ceremony uniting the king and the god was conducted. Carvings of *devatas*,

1 *Angkor Wat at dawn. On the equinox, the sun rises directly over the tower of the central sanctuary.*

central sanctuary housed an image of Shiva, the god with whom the king was said to be one. Three concentric galleries enclose the central sanctuary, rising as one approaches the center of the complex. The stairway

female deities, appear throughout the temple, and the galleries display scenes from the ancient Indian epic the *Mahabharata*, as well as other Hindu myths, heightening the drama of this holy citadel.

2 *All within the enclosure of Angkor Wat is still dark and silent as the first glimmers of light in the eastern sky illuminate the silhouettes of the five towers, which cast their shadows onto the sacred pond.*

3 *Looking down on Angkor Wat, surrounded by dense tropical forest, from the heights of Phnom Kulen.*

4 *Elephants walking along the ancient royal road. Elephants were an important part of the Angkor army, used in carrying weapons and supplies and also as mounts in battle. Many such scenes appear in bas-reliefs at Angkor sites.*

5 *Cows bathing in the moat surrounding Angkor Wat. In India, Hindus regard white cows as sacred, and they worship and revere them. This custom survives in Cambodia today.*

6 *The main concourse leading to Angkor Wat is paved with thick, square-cut stones. It is 12 meters wide and 540 meters long. The stone balustrades on both sides are in the shape of the snake deity, or naga.*

7 Bright touches of color remain on the pillars and the ceiling of the cruciform passageway connecting the first and second galleries, allowing us a glimpse of the brilliance of the structure at the height of Angkor's glory.

8 Buddha images stand on the four sides of the central sanctuary, the largest of the five towers.
These were placed here after the fall of Angkor, when Angkor Wat became a Buddhist temple.

9 *The roof of the third gallery is sculpted with figures of ascetics practicing austerities, legs crossed, eyes closed in meditation, and hands in a gesture of reverence. Ascetics in a similar style can be seen in Angkor-period sites in Thailand and Laos.*

10 *The highest section of Angkor Wat is a square, with the main sanctuary rising in its center. Galleries run around its exterior and cut the square into four smaller squares, each of which is a bathing pool where devotees purified themselves before worshiping.*

11 A devata *from the exterior of the west gate of Angkor Wat. She wears an elaborate headdress* *and neckpiece, and she holds a flower. The narrow, slanted eyes and heavy lips are distinctive.*

12 *The first gallery is two hundred meters on a side. The walls of each gallery are filled with reliefs depicting scenes from such Indian epics at the* Mahabharata *and the* Ramayana, *and events from the history of the Angkor empire.*

13 Suryavarman II, who built Angkor Wat, is depicted on the west side of the south wall of the first gallery. He is seated on a throne in the shape of a naga, surrounded by many parasols and fans.

14 An image of the god Vishnu at the northwest corner of the first gallery. Suryavarman II wished to be reborn as Vishnu, and had the same face sculpted for his portrait and that of the god.

15 A section of the "Heaven and Hell" scenes from the east side of the south wall of the first gallery. In this section from a "Heaven" scene, a princess parts with the queen at lower left. Royal processions are also visible.

16 Bas-relief devata on the outer wall of the second gallery. Though the figures are set against plain backgrounds, their elaborate hairstyles, head ornaments, and gestures, each unique, are testimony to the richness of the aesthetic vocabulary of Khmer court culture.

17 *These graceful figures of devata* appear at the entrance to the central sanctuary, the highest of the five towers at Angkor Wat. The *eyes of the figures are closed in meditation, and the linking of the figures with those on other walls creates a sense of perspective.*

18 A devata *near the entrance to the central sanctuary. Her direct gaze, the supple gesture with which she holds a flower stem, and the richly ornamental carving are perfectly harmonious and filled with a heavenly refinement.*

19 Angkor Wat is particularly beautiful at sunset. As the last rays of the setting sun move across the monument, they illuminate the reliefs, decorations, windows, and bays with ever-changing patterns of light and darkness.

20 *The traditional dance of Cambodia has been revived in recent years, as the devata depicted on the walls of Angkor Wat are reborn. The lithe, unhurried, and controlled movements of the dancers clearly echo the poses of the ancient bas-relief figures.*

ANGKOR THOM AND BAYON TEMPLE

Jayavarman VII carried out successful campaigns to pacify and unite the Angkor domains and he also significantly increased them by conquest. He built the network of royal roads, and linked them all to Angkor Thom, the new capital of the empire, which he built from the end of the twelfth to the beginning of the thirteenth century. The city was three kilometers on a side and was surrounded by a moat more than one hundred meters wide. Five huge gates led into the city from north, east, south, and west. The ruins of many structures are to be found within the city: Bayon Temple, the Elephants Terrace, the Terrace of the Leper King, and many other buildings from Jayavarman VII's time, as well as those from the tenth century, including Phimeanakas and Baphuon temples, and the royal palace. A large open space in front of the Elephants Terrace was reserved for the king to review his troops as they left on their expeditions of conquest and upon their victorious return. Jayavarman VII was the first of the Angkor kings to be a follower of Buddhism, and he built the Bayon Temple in the center of the city as a symbol of Mount Sumeru, the center of the world in Buddhist cosmology. Bayon is a Mahayana Buddhist temple dedicated to spreading compassion through the "three thousand worlds" of the universe. Battles between Khmer forces and the Chams are depicted in the bas-reliefs of the first gallery. Other reliefs show scenes of everyday life, such as markets, food preparation, cockfights, and fortunetellers, offering a vivid depiction of the richness of the everyday lives of the inhabitants of the Angkor kingdom during the illustrious reign of the great builder-king Jayavarman VII.

21 *The south gate of Angkor Thom bears a carving of the face of the bodhisattva Avalokiteshvara.*

22 Leaving Angkor Wat from its western exit and heading north, one arrives at Angkor Thom's south gate. A causeway leads to the gate. Statues of giants holding a huge naga line both sides of the causeway.

23 *Avalokiteshvara looks down over those who enter the south gate. The gate tower is two hundred meters high, and the bodhisattva's faces, on all four sides of the tower, are about three meters in height.*

24 *The giant statues along both sides of the causeway leading to the south gate form two rows:* devas *on the left and* ashuras *on the right. The figures on both sides are holding a* naga.

25 *Bayon Temple has fifty-four towers with faces of Avalokiteshvara carved on four sides.
It is built as a pyramid, gradually rising to the central sanctuary, forty-five meters high.*

26 *Bayon is unique among all Angkor-period ruins in its construction. The faces of Avalokiteshvara have been carved into huge blocks of stone hoisted into position, creating an aesthetic of overwhelming force and boldness.*

27 *The pillars of the south side of the first gallery cast shadows across the reliefs that fill the gallery's outer walls. The pillars once supported a roof.*

28 Many reliefs at Bayon depict battles between the Khmers and the Chams. This scene shows a boat of Chams attacking the Khmer forces. The twenty oarsmen and warriors with spears and shields are depicted with exciting realism.

29 Cham soldiers on the attack. They wear lotus-blossom shaped helmets and brandish spears and shields in this dynamic and powerful depiction of waving arms and stamping, jostling feet.

30 *The defending Khmer forces, with an officer drawing his bow from the back of an elephant. In sharp contrast to the heavily armored Cham soldiers they trample underfoot, the Khmer soldiers wear no helmets, are barefoot, and are naked except for a decorative belt.*

31 *Baphuon, just to the north of Bayon, was built by Udayadityavarman II in the mid-eleventh century. It was the main royal temple of the period, and taller than Bayon.*

32 *Phimeanakas was built in the early eleventh century from laterite stacked in three layers, in pyramid fashion. Known as the "Temple above the Clouds," the ceremony in which divinity was conferred upon the king was conducted in the sanctuary at its apex.*

33 *The road from the terrace of the palace to the Victory Gate. Two rows of twelve tower structures called* khleang *stand on either side of the road. The king reviewed his forces from here when setting out on a royal procession or sending troops off to battle.*

34 *The Terrace of Elephants is over three meters tall and is carved with a long line of elephants.*

35 *Three martial deities with weapons held aloft and legs spread wide, sculpted on a narrow interior wall near the terrace of the royal palace.*

36 *The faces of Avalokiteshvara carved on the four sides of the towers take on different expressions, sometimes forbidding, sometimes gentle and compassionate, with the changing light of sunset.*

37 Monks conducting a religious ceremony at a Buddhist sanctuary on the west side of Bayon. Suppressed in recent years, Cambodian Buddhism is reviving and Buddhist services are held in many locations on the day of the full moon.

38 Bayon is a Buddhist temple. There are several Buddhist sanctuaries in the vicinity, and Buddhist monks and lay believers often visit them. The rain has just stopped, and monks are resting in front of Bayon after a ceremony conducted at the temple.

39 *Traveling through the forests of Angkor. Most of the monuments built at the peak of the Angkor empire are concentrated near Siem Reap. The royal roads cut through the forests, linking one edifice to another, still exist today.*

RUINS FROM THE EARLY DAYS
OF THE ANGKOR KINGDOM

Angkor emerged as a unified kingdom when the capital was moved from the lower reaches of the Mekong River to the area known today as Siem Reap. In 802, Jayavarman II crowned himself first king of Angkor at Phnom Kulen, or Mount Kulen. From that time on, the foundations of the Angkor empire were established with this area as the kingdom's center. In

East Mebon, and Pre Rup. In this period, the main structure of temples was built from bricks, with laterite used for the base and exterior walls and sandstone for lintels and false doors. Banteay Srei, one of the best representatives of temple architecture of this period, was built from pink sandstone. The many highly detailed relief carvings decorating all its surfaces are of

40 *Bakong is a five-story pyramid temple, the first to be built from blocks of sandstone.*

877, the first capital was built in what is now Roluoh, and two temples dedicated to Shiva, Preah Koh and Bakong, were built. Later the capital was moved to Yasodaharapura (modern Phnom Bakheng), and in the eighth century, many temples were built in the area around the capital, including Prasat Kravan, Baksei Chamkrong, the

high quality, and can be fairly described as the greatest masterpieces among all surviving ancient Angkor sites. The late French writer André Malraux was so enchanted by an image of a *devata* here that he stole it—a story he recounts in his novel set in the ruins of Angkor, *Le Voie Royale* (The Royal Road).

41 *The road to Bakong is much as it was when first built centuries ago, and the scenes of daily life visible along it are reflected in the reliefs of the temples it connects.*

42 Bakong was built in 881 by Indravarman and dedicated to Shiva. It is the first temple to be surrounded by a moat, and it had a great stylistic and structural influence on the construction of Angkor Wat.

43 *Preah Koh means "Sacred Bull," and a stone image of the sacred bull Nandi, vehicle of Shiva, stands before the temple's central sanctuary. Jayavarman I built Preah Koh in 879 for his parents.*

44 *Rajendravarman II built Baksei Chamkrong in 948. It is a simple temple, with a four-story base topped by a tower. Rajendravarman II went on to build the East Mebon and Pre Rup.*

45 *Prasat Kravan is a Hindu temple built by Harshavarman I in 921. Five sanctuaries stood on a long horizontal base, and three figures of Vishnu were sculpted in relief on the walls of the central sanctuary.*

46 An eight-armed Vishnu figure on the wall of the central sanctuary of
Prasat Kravan, against a background of hundreds of his incarnations.

47 *Pre Rup is a pyramid temple built in 961 by Rajendravarman II. It closely resembles East Mebon in shape and style. The tall central sanctuary flanked by four towers sits atop a high, three-story base.*

48 *Rajendravarman II built east Mebon for his ancestors. Lion statues stand on both side of the stairway leading up to the central sanctuary, and the brick towers are situated in a balanced, symmetrical layout, equal to Pre Rup in beauty.*

49 *The approach to Banteay Srei, a Shiva temple about three hundred meters northeast of Angkor Wat. Built in 967, Banteay Srei is distinguished by its* devatas *and many reliefs, beautifully and elegantly sculpted in sandstone.*

50 The "library" on the north side of Banteay Srei is completely covered in decorative and narrative carvings. A scene from the *Mahabharata is sculpted on the pediment over the doorway.*

51 Six beautiful devatas are sculpted on the north walls of the sanctuaries on both sides of the central sanctuary. This voluptuous beauty wears a single flower in her hair and an earring in a floral design.

52 In a scene from the Indian epic the Ramayana, the demon king Rawana attempts to carry off Princess Sita. From a lintel on the west wall of the central sanctuary at Banteay Srei.

53 *Children playing near a waterwheel in the Siem Reap River which begins in the Phnom Kulen highlands and flows into the Great Lake.*

TRACES OF THE ANGKOR KINGDOM
BURIED IN THE JUNGLE

The Dangrek Mountains stretch across the northernmost edge of Cambodia, marking its border with Thailand. On a cliff near that border stands Preah Vihear, built at the beginning of the eleventh century. Behind the central sanctuary dedicated to Shiva a sheer cliff rises six hundred meters. In front, a sea of green rainforest unfolds to the horizon. On a clear day, the mountains of Phnom Kulen and the Tonle Sap,

the capital are such temple ruins as Bayon, Ta Prohm, Preah Khan, and Banteay Kdei. Ta Prohm is an example of a temple that was discovered in the midst of the jungle, untouched since it was abandoned. Massive tree roots, like huge serpents, crawl over the roof and walls, testimony to the amazing life force of the jungle. Looking at these ancient ruins, one can't help but be impressed by the power of nature and the weight

54 The roots of a banyan tree spreading over the roof of the gallery at Ta Prohm temple reveal the tremendous living force of the rain forest.

the Great Lake, are visible. Jayavarman VII acceded to the throne in 1181 and immediately began to reign with vigor from his new capital of Angkor Thom. He sought to use Buddhism to unify the kingdom, and he had many temples built along the royal roads. Within and in close proximity to

of history. There are many ruins—perhaps even on a scale similar to Angkor Wat—still slumbering peacefully in the tropical forests of Cambodia, long inaccessible because of the warfare that has wracked the nation for so many years. They cry out for immediate survey and restoration work.

55 *The Preah Vihear temple complex is in the Dangrek Mountains on the Thai border, which lies at the foot of this stairway. The steep approach to the main sanctuary passes through three large gates and is 840 meters long.*

56 *The main sanctuary at Preah Vihear sits at the very back of a low slope, with a sheer and impassable six-hundred-meter cliff behind it. The temple is best visited from the Thai side of the border.*

57 *Preah Vihear was first built as a wooden temple by Yasovarman I, and later kings added to the complex. The present stone structure was built during the reign of Suryavarman I. This is a portion of the gallery near the third gate.*

58 *The structure at the top of the stairs in the center of the photograph is the remains of the first gate. The large naga to the right is more naturalistic than the stylized nagas of Angkor, resembling a giant cobra slithering over the ground.*

59 *Thai soldiers standing at the border in the Dangrek Mountains. The mountain drops five or six hundred meters just beyond the bamboo fence. The Dangrek range stretches off to the left, and below it lie the tropical forests of Cambodia.*

60 *A sudden squall passes over the forests of northern Cambodia in this view from the heights of the Dangrek Mountains in Thailand, looking over the forest toward Siem Reap. Many ruins of the Angkor period remain hidden in the dense jungle.*

61 *Ta Keo was built in the early eleventh century, but construction was stopped halfway after the death of the king. The stone blocks of the temple were assembled but no relief carvings were sculpted. As a result, it has a bold and simple beauty all its own.*

62 Banteay Samre was built in the mid-twelfth century by Suryavarman II. "Banteay" means "citadel," and this temple complex is surrounded by high, thick walls. There is also a moat (now dry) around the central sanctuary.

63 *Galleries and the roofs of many sanctuaries at Preah Kahn.*

64 *A temple gallery and a heap of cut stones. The monks' quarters and galleries linking the many sanctuaries are buried in rubble.*

65 *Dancing asparas sculpted on a gallery pillar. Cambodian court dance has preserved similar postures and gestures to this very day.*

66 *Preah Kahn is a Buddhist temple, built by Jayavarman VII at the end of the eleventh century. The temple is just as it was when rediscovered, with the roots of banyan trees spread over its roofs and galleries, and heaps of fallen stone.*

67 *This devata from a hidden corner of Ta Prohm is not as sophisticated and elegant as the devatas at Angkor Wat, but is charming nonetheless for the artless simplicity and immediacy of its expression.*

68 *The outer wall of Ta Prohm near the main gate, and the ancient road passing*
in front of the complex. Jayavarman VII built this temple in 1186 for his mother.

69 *A banyan tree growing over the entry to a gallery leading to a sanctuary tower (at right). No restoration efforts have been undertaken at Ta Prohm, and it remains today just as it was when discovered in the jungle.*

70 A heap of stones in the central courtyard of Ta Prohm, surrounded by the walls of a gallery. Beautifully
stylized images of devatas are sculpted in the panels between the false windows lining the gallery.

71 Banteay Kdei is a Hindu temple built at the end of the twelfth century. It was later rebuilt as a Buddhist
temple by Jayavarman VII. Most Khmer buildings were added to by successive dynasties of kings.

72 *The Srah Srang pool at daybreak. "Srah Srang" means "royal bath." Two lions stand guard at the steps leading down into the pool and the stone balustrades on either side of the steps end in nagas. Jayavarman VII built this royal bath at the end of the twelfth century.*

73 A seated Buddha image at Banteay Kdei. Jayavarman VII was an avid devotee of Buddhism and built many Buddhist temples throughout his domains. This image was missing its head, and after being restored has been returned to life by the floral offerings of devotees.

THE ORIGINS OF ANGKOR AND THE GREAT MEKONG BASIN

Pakxè is a town in southern Laos that has flourished since ancient times as an important transportation center. South from Pakxè is the town of Champasak. Proceeding south from Champasak, one arrives at Khone Falls, at the border with Cambodia. Wat Phu, a Khmer ruin, lies at the foot of a mountain outside Champasak. As the name suggests, this region was once under the rule of the Champa kingdom, and a

is regarded as the original homeland of the Khmers. As they grew in strength, they gradually began to push south along the Mekong River, until in the early seventh century they established their capital of Ishanapura, about thirty kilometers north of modern Kompong Thom. From here they expanded their territory to include most of modern Cambodia, southern Vietnam, southeast Thailand, and parts of the

74 *A bamboo bridge leading to an island in the Mekong River in Kompong Cham where vegetables are cultivated.*

Cham Hindu temple originally occupied the site of Wat Phu. In the sixth and seventh centuries, the Khmers conquered the region, and from that time the Wat Phu complex was rebuilt and added to several times. The surviving buildings were constructed in the eleventh century. Champasak

Malay Penninsula, creating as they did so a unified Khmer Empire. Today Sambor Prei Kuk, located at the site of the ancient capital of Ishanapura, survives here'. Consisting of three groups of brick structures, it is the source of the beautiful and sophisticated Sambor style of architecture and sculpture.

75 *Children playing in the Mekong River near Pakxé, which has been an important urban center in southern Laos from ancient times. The Mekong is wide and relatively shallow here, making boat travel possible all year round. It is also an important fishery.*

76 Vendors selling Laotian-style noodles on a ferry boat to Champasak.

77 The ferryboat trip from Pakxé to Champasak takes about three hours. Water buffaloes ride along with the passengers.

78 *Wat Phu at Champasak. As the name indicates, this was once part of Cham territory. The white cham flower, symbolic of the Cham people, is in bloom at left. Two palaces and several reservoirs can be seen, and, in the distance, the Mekong River.*

79 A portion of the gallery of the "men's palace," the best-preserved structure at the site. This region came under the control of the Khmer people of the Chenla kingdom in the fifth century, and additional construction was carried out under successive Khmer rulers.

80 The palace known as "the women's palace" at Wat Phu. A concourse leads between the two palaces, continuing.up a flight of stairs to the central sanctuary. Mount Pasak rises in the background.

81 A false door, with lintel and pediment, in the men's palace. Shiva, seated on his
vehicle, the sacred bull Nandi, is depicted in the central section of the pediment.

82 Khone Falls, at the border of Laos and Cambodia, are ten kilometers long. The Khmer Chenla was centered on Champasak, and in the fifth century began to expand southward along the Mekong, eventually extending throughout the plains of Cambodia.

83 *The Sen River as it flows through Kompong Thom. After moving down from Champasak, the Khmer-Chenla people built a capital at Kompong Thom from the sixth through the seventh century, gradually claiming a broad territory in eastern and central Cambodia.*

84 In November, after the rice harvest, temporary pavilions are set up in the fields and the monks are invited to dine. Cambodian Buddhists believe they acquire merit by making offerings to temples and monks.

85 After decades of religious oppression, the Cambodian people are once again able to practice their faith. From ancient times, religion has played a major role in their daily lives.

86 *The first sanctuary of the north site at Sambor Prei Kuk, some thirty kilometers to the north of the city of Kompong Thom. This was the capital of the Khmer Chenla kingdom in the latter half of the sixth century.*

87 A relief from the fifteenth sanctuary at Sambor Prei Kuk. The relief sculpture on the brick surface closely resembles those of Cham sites. The two monsters, makara, on either side of the human figure at the top are sometimes seen at Angkor sites.

88 *Children driving oxen home at sunset in a field outside Kompong Thom. The sugar palm rising in the center is an ancient symbol of Cambodia. They are often found growing nearby ancient Angkor sites in Thailand as well.*

89 *Banners at the entrance to the temple at the peak of Phnom Sandak. The mountain has been regarded as a holy site since ancient times, and there are many meditation caves near the peak.*

90 *The ancient pilgrimage road as seen from atop Phnom Sandak. It leads to National Highway 6, heading off to the ancient Angkor capital of Siem Reap to the west and Kompong Cham and Phnom Penh to the east.*

91 *Wat Nokor in Kompong Cham was built as a Buddhist temple in the eleventh century. The central sanctuary is surrounded by four towers, and a high wall encloses the entire group. A modern Buddhist temple has been built adjacent to the central sanctuary.*

92 *Lions and nagas stand guard before the entranceway to Wat Nokor. The gateway closely resembles that of Banteay Kdei, built in the twelfth century, but the devatas and other sculptural images are not as decoratively elaborate.*

93 Wat Nokor is built from a distinctive black sandstone. This scene from a pediment on the south side of the central
sanctuary shows the Buddha taking the tonsure (above) and leaving the palace on his beloved mount Kanthaka.

94 *In the evening, the local people gather at the Mekong River near Kompong Cham to swim and enjoy the cool breezes. National Highway 7 intersects with the Mekong in Kompong Cham, which has been an important crossroads since ancient times.*

95 *A bamboo bridge at sunset. All of the bridges to islands in the Mekong are made*
of bamboo, and they are strong enough to allow the passage of large trucks.

96 *Oxcarts remain a necessity in Cambodian farming villages. Carts identical to these can be seen in the reliefs at Bayon.*

97 *National Highway 2, leading to Ta Keo, was once the road leading to, Angkor Borei, the capital of Funan.*

98 *Cham children catching fish. A Cham village of about two hundred exists in the countryside near Ta Keo.*

99 *Tonle Bati temple is on the right side of National Highway 2, about thirty kilometers from Phnom Penh on the way to Ta Keo. It is a small temple, but is frequently visited because of its proximity to Phnom Penh.*

100 *The entrance gate and, atop the mountain at right, Phnom Chisor. A Hindu temple built in the eleventh century, it is sparsely decorated but dynamic in its layout, with its two large gates and a long, straight concourse leading directly up to the temple above.*

101 A cowherd walking along the road leading to Phnom Chisor. Passing through the collapsed gate at the foot of the slope, one proceeds up a steep laterite stairway leading up to the main hall of the temple, which was built in the early eleventh century by Suryavarman II.

102 *Looking down at the concourse leading to Phnom Chisor from atop the hill. The road leads from the gate in the foreground in a straight line out to the outer gate, past the reservoirs, and on to the ancient capital Angkor Borei.*

103 *Phnom Bayang stands on the peak to the left. Traces of an ancient laterite stairway that once led up to the temple remain scattered around the area. There is a cave halfway up the smaller peak at the right that has been used as a place of meditation from ancient times.*

104 *The reliefs on the southern face of the temple bear a close resemblance to those of the fifteenth sanctuary at Sambor Prei Kuk in Kompong Thom. Depictions of an Indian epic grace the central false door and the two panels on either side.*

105 A road leads along the left side of the central temple of Phnom Bayang. A new Buddhist image has been installed in the interior worship hall and is visited by worshipers today.

106 *The view from atop Phnom Bayang. Reservoirs and irrigation systems were always built nearby ancient Angkor sites, making it possible to grow two rice crops in the vicinity. In other regions of Cambodia, the dry season made this impossible.*

The Road from Champa to Angkor

The kingdom of Champa flourished from the second through the fifteenth century in what is today central and southern Vietnam. Many Cham ruins survive in this area, of which Mi Son, a center of religious activity, is perhaps the most representative. The Chams made their first at-tempt to invade Angkor in 1177. They attacked by land, and they failed. For their next at-tempt they formed a huge naval fleet and sailed up the Mekong River to the Great Lake, attacking Angkor from the lake's north-west corner and succeeding in occupying the region. From that time on the two forces engaged in repeated battles, which are dramatically represented in great detail in the bas-reliefs of Bayon Temple. In the fifteenth century, attacks on Champa by Vietnamese forces from the north gradually led to the kingdom's destruc-tion. Most of the Cham people fled to other Southeast Asian countries, where they were assimilated into the local populations. A small number of Chams survive in Vietnam today. The descendants of this proud people, who once threatened the many kingdoms near to the Mekong and the Great Lake, and flourished through maritime trade, now live quietly as fishermen. Most modern Chams are followers of Islam. The Mekong and the Great Lake still function today as a well-developed network of "water roads" as important in both trade and war as they were in the days of ancient Angkor.

107 The "elephant-tusk" towers were influenced by the three-tower style of Khmer architecture.

108 Mi Son, the religious center of the Champa kingdom, is located on a plain surrounded by mountains. It is a quiet, isolated location with a strongly sacred atmosphere. The structures here were built from the eighth through the thirteenth centuries, added to and rebuilt repeatedly.

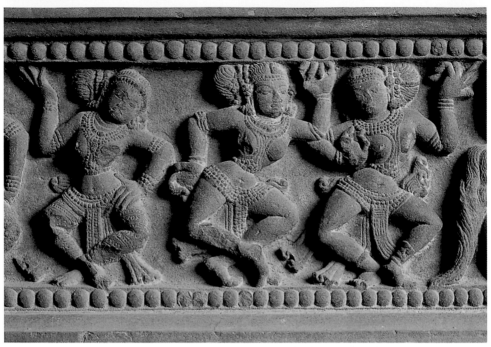

109 *Dancers excavated at Tra Kieu (Indrapura), the capital of the Chams from the fourth through the eighth centuries. Many fine works of sculpture have been unearthed at this site. The movement of the dancers' arms and legs is beautifully expressed.*

110 *A flute player from an altar at Mi Son. Cham civilization reached its peak in the eighth to ninth centuries.*

111 *An elegant and refined dancer (aspara) from the late tenth century, unearthed atTra Kieu.*

112 *The elephant-tusk towers were built in the twelfth century. The brick and the nagas sculpted in the sandstone pediments are characteristic.*

113 A group of Chams, descendants of the rulers of the ancient Champa kingdom, live in a village outside Phan Rang. With the collapse of the Cham empire, its people dispersed across Asia. Some twenty thousand Chams live in Vietnam today.

114 Many Chams live in villages specializing in pottery
and textile production. This village makes unglazed pots.

115 Some Chams still practice their ancient religion. A
monk holds a religious text written in the Cham script.

116 A water market on the Mekong outside the city of Cantho in the Mekong Delta. The soil of the Mekong Delta is rich, and it is the "rice basket" of Vietnam. Every day, markets all over the region offer fresh vegetables, fruits, fish, and shellfish.

117 *Rice paddies near the important archeological site Oc Eo, an important trading port of the kingdom of Funan. Artifacts from as far away as Rome and India were discovered at this site on the southern coast of Vietnam.*

118 *Fishing in a tributary of the Mekong. There are many navigable rivers and streams near Oc Eo, which owed its development as a trading center to this network of waterways.*

119 *Phnom Da is in Cambodia, about one hundred kilometers northwest of Oc Eo. It was built in the seventh century from laterite. Sculptures from the sixth and seventh centuries, as well as the oldest Khmer stele inscription, were discovered here.*

120 *The stone temple Ashram Maha Rosei is located about halfway up the small mountain Phnom Bakheng, which is adjacent to the sacred mountain Phnom Da. A Harihara statue, a combination of Shiva on the right and Vishnu on the left, was discovered at this small shrine.*

121 *A well-developed irrigation system is evident in this view from the top of Phnom Da. In the dry season, the paddies are blanketed in green. Houses are visible among the trees in the foreground.*

122 *The Chau Doc River flowing through Angkor Borei. This was the site of the capital of Funan after its retreat from the Khmer Chenla forces pressing down from the north. Many Buddhist and Hindu images have been unearthed in this area.*

123 *A group of Chams have built homes on the raised banks of the Great Lake near Phnom Penh and make their living fishing the lake. In the early eleventh century, Champa armies advanced up the Tonle Sap River to attack and occupy Angkor.*

124 *When the Chams were eventually defeated by the Vietnamese, many fled to Cambodia.*
Their descendants are followers of Islam, and they retain their cultural identity to this day.

125 *Cambodians, Vietnamese, and Chams live in houseboats on the Tonle Sap River as it flows through Kompong Chhnang. Most make their living fishing the Great Lake. This area has prospered as an important nexus of water transportation since ancient times.*

126 *The Great Lake is known as one of the world's richest sources of freshwater fish. Fisherman set sail in their small boats at daybreak. The bas-reliefs at Bayon depict fishermen on the lake, as well as naval battles of Khmer and Cham armies.*

127 Many Cambodians, Vietnamese, and Chams live on houseboats in the area where the Siem Reap River flows into the Great Lake.

128 Siem Reap, where Angkor is located, is about fifteen kilometers from the Great Lake. The road runs parallel to the Siem Reap River.

129 *Houses on stilts along the road from the Great Lake to the Angkor capital. During the rainy season the lake doubles in size, and only the road remains above water. From ancient times, the road has been a pathway of both trade and conquest.*

THE SACRED SITES OF ANGKOR IN THAILAND

After Suryavarman I pacified the Khmer kingdom, which had long been plagued by internal strife, he expanded Angkor's territory as far as Lopburi in Thailand and built Preah Vihear atop the Dangrek Mountains. Suryavarman II carried out military campaigns in Thailand to further expand the network of royal roads. Many of the main Angkor sites in Thailand were built at this time. Jayavarman VII, the Buddhist discovered in the largest Khmer site in Thailand, Phimai. During Jayavarman's reign, the temple changed from a Hindu to a Mahayana Buddhist temple, and several Bayon-style Buddhist images have been discovered there. There are also many Khmer ruins in the vicinity of Surin and Brinam in northeastern Thailand. These lay along the route of the royal road leading from the capital of Angkor to Phimai and Sukhotai,

130 *At the end of November, when the rice harvest is finished, these Thai farmers celebrate a festival in which they present the fruits of their labors to the temple.*

monarch who built Bayon, extended Angkor's rule into the Chaya region of southern Thailand, marking the summit of the kingdom's glory. A statue of Jayavarman VII has been the first independentThai kingdom. Large numbers of people of Khmer descent live in this region, and the older generation still speaks Khmer.

131 *The Qoi people, original inhabitants of Thailand, have always hunted elephants in the forests of Cambodia, trained them, and sold them as a living. Famed as elephant handlers, they supplied the riders for the war-elephant troops of the ancient Khmer and Thai armies.*

132 Phnom Rung is a Hindu temple built atop a 170-meter mountain from the late eleventh to the early twelfth century. It occupied an important place as a midway point between the Khmer capital and Phimai temple.

133 *The south wall of the anteroom to the central sanctuary. This complex contains many pediments of the type seen here. They depict Shiva dancing, Shiva mounted on the sacred bull Nandi, and scenes from the* Ramayana.

134 *Young monks visiting Phnom Rung. Up to the beginning of the thirteenth century, this remained an active center of Hindu faith, but when Angkor lost its Thai territories, the influence of Theravada Buddhism predominated.*

135 *The pediment on the west side of the main sanctuary at Phnom Rung depicts a scene from the Ramayana.*
Sita rests inside a temple in the center, surrounded by multiple depictions of the monkey god, Hanuman.

136 *The central sanctuary of Phnom Rung. A gallery links an anteroom to the main sancturay. The tower is cruciform, the pediments above its four entrances extending up toward the central sanctuary in a depiction of an idealized heavenly city.*

137 *Cowherds along the ancient road outside Surin. The regions around Surin and Buriram in northeast Thailand were once Angkor territories, and numerous remains from that period survive. Many ethnic Khmers live here, and the older generations still speak Khmer.*

138 *Prasat Muang Tam is located two or three kilometers below Phnom Rung, on the same hill. A sacred pond surrounds the temple, which is compact and quite lovely. A large rectangular reservoir from the Angkor period is located next to the site.*

139 *At Muang Tam, three sanctuaries are enclosed by galleries in an unusual layout scheme. The main pillars and lintels of the brick entrances to the sanctuaries are made of sandstone and are beautifully sculpted.*

140 *The lintel stone of the entry to one of the sanctuaries at Muang Tam depicts Shiva and his consort riding Shiva's mount, the sacred bull Nandi. The powerfully sculpted demon beneath the main figures is a protective deity.*

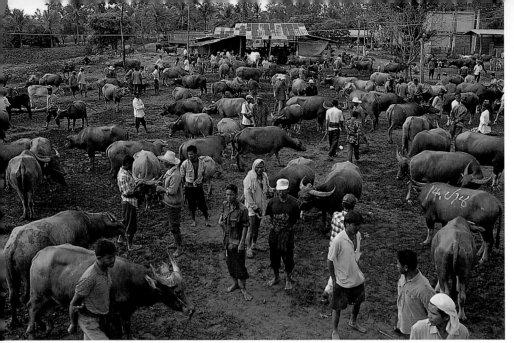

141 *A water buffalo market in northeastern Thailand near Sisaket. Thai farmers still rely on the buffaloes to plow their fields. They are an important possession, and many families raise them.*

142 *Oxcarts heaped with large loads arriving home from the fields. Water buffaloes are a common sight all over Southeast Asia and farmers depend heavily upon them.*

143 *A timeless scene along an ancient road outside of Buriram in northeastern Thailand. A farm girl makes her way home after a day in the fields. The red clay roads once so typical of the region have all but disappeared.*

144 In April, the hottest month of the dry season, farmers hold festivals and ceremonies to pray for a successful harvest. Boat races are regarded as a rain-making ritual. Each hamlet selects oarsmen to participate and win good fortune for the local area.

145 In the rocket festival held at Sisaket in northeastern Thailand, bamboo rockets are launched from a ladder tied to a tree. This festival, popular in northeastern Thailand and Laos, is held in mid-April to ensure a bountiful harvest and thriving progeny.

146 *Sikhoraphum is a Hindu temple built at the start of the eleventh century. It is unique in that each of its five brick sanctuary towers is shaped differently from the others. The pillar and lintel sculptures of the main sanctuary are especially beautiful.*

147 *A ten-armed Shiva dances in the center of the lintel carving of the central sanctuary. The other walls of the sanctuary are completely covered with depictions of Vishnu and Parvati, Ganesha, dancing asparas, and other Hindu figures.*

148 *The pillars supporting the pediment of the entrance to the central sanctuary, with a naga above.*

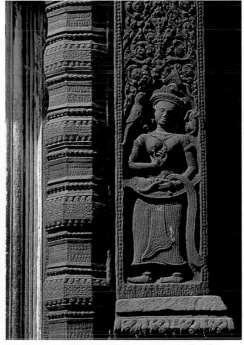

149 *The carving of the main pillars and octagonal pillars that support the pediment of the entry to the main sanctuary.*

150 *Phimai is a Hindu temple built by Jayavarman VI in the early eleventh century. An Esoteric Buddhist image enshrined as the main object of worship suggests that it became a Mahayana Buddhist temple during the reign of Jayavarman VII.*

151 *Some four hundred fifty meters of galleries surround the central sanctuary. These sandstone pillars mark a section of the cruciform gallery leading to the processional route from the south gate (to the left). The galleries were once roofed in the same style as Angkor Wat.*

152 *Relief carvings on the exterior wall of the central sanctuary at Phimai, with stylized scrolled flowers and lotus buds. These motifs are widely used in contemporary Thai temple architecture, crafts, and design.*

153 *Thai boy monks. Thailand requires six years of compulsory education, but many Thai families are too poor to allow their children to attend secondary school. Many temples run schools, allowing students to continue with their studies as they practice their religion.*

154 *The boy monks spend an hour in the early morning begging, then return to the temple to study religion in the morning and school subjects in the afternoon. After graduating, some remain behind as monks but others go on to work as civil servants or in the private sector.*

155 *Dusk over the Mun River, which flows alongside Phimai. The area around Phimai, crisscrossed with canals and dotted with ponds fed by the sacred river, retains the atmosphere of centuries gone by.*

156 *Prang Sam Yod, near Lopburi Station, is an ancient Khmer site with three tower sanctuaries made from brick and sandstone. Though it lacks sculpture or reliefs, a very important eleventh-century Khmer stele inscription was discovered here.*

157 *Muang Singh, the Khmer site farthest to the northwest, was built by Jayavarman VII. A Buddhist temple enshrining Avalokiteshvara, it is much visited today.*

158 *Jayavarman VII had many images of Avalokitshvara sculpted and enshrined in the main sanctuary of Muang Singh.* 153
They are distinguished by the single seated Buddha on the head and small seated Buddhas sculpted in relief on the bare torso.

159 *Wat Si Sanpat, a typical Ayutthaya-style Buddhist temple, was built at the beginning of the fifteenth century by Ramathibodhi II. Many temples were constructed at this time, the peak of the Ayutthaya empire's prosperity.*

160 *The Great Buddha of Wat Chelum, on the outskirts of Ayutthaya, is nineteen meters in height. The seated image is made of bronze and was completed in 1350. Though the Ayutthaya kingdom had only recently been established, this image is powerful and commanding.*

161 A seated Ayùtthaya-period Buddha beneath a bodhi tree at Wat Mahathat. The expression of calm introspection
contrasts sharply with the image at Wat Chelum. It seems to be an image sculpted in a time of peace.

162 *Siamese troops depicted in the first gallery at Angkor Wat. After the death of Jayavarman VII in the early thirteenth century, the Angkor empire entered a period of decline and Siamese forces became a growing threat.*

163 An Elephant Festival is held every year in mid-November in the town of Surin in northeastern Thailand. A procession of the "king" and his warriors dressed in ancient costume fills the festival grounds.

164 In the fourteenth century, Ayutthaya became a strong and independent kingdom, repeatedly attacking Angkor. At the end of the fifteenth century, it sent a large force to Angkor's capital and conquered it, assimilating a large part of western Cambodia.

165 *After conquering Angkor, Ayutthaya enjoyed four centuries of glory, but was devastated by a Burmese invasion in 1767. Afterward, the capital was moved first to to Thonburi and then Bangkok, the present capital.*

ALL ROYAL ROADS LEAD TO ANGKOR

ALL ROYAL ROADS LEAD TO ANGKOR

By Yoshiaki Ishizawa

KHMER SOCIETY

The emergence and development of Angkor civilization was dependent upon the Mekong River. Its seasonal flooding made for rich agricultural harvests on the land along its banks, and it is a plentiful source of fish. Cambodia has a monsoon climate, with alternating dry seasons and rainy seasons. The red soil of the central Cambodian plains contains large amounts of iron, and is not particularly well suited to agriculture. Yet the Khmer people built one of the world's great civilizations on this relatively infertile land.

The ancient Khmer people were light-skinned, with prominent features. They possessed a special form of hemoglobin E that may have made them resistant to malaria. Their language belongs to the Mon-Khmer family and is monosyllabic, unvoiced, and complex in grammar and syntax. Their numerical system only goes up to five.

From ancient times, the inhabitants of Cambodia have shared a distinct and identifiable physical culture, one that in large part persists today. The sarong is the national form of dress, and the staple diet consists of fermented fish paste and boiled rice. The typical Cambodian house is a rectangular structure of post-and-beam construction made of wood and palm leaves. The floor is suspended about two meters above the ground from the pillars that support the roof. One enters by climbing a rough wooden ladder that always has an uneven number of steps. Such elevated houses are common throughout the Cambodian countryside

even today. Contrary to the common assumption, they are not built off the ground to protect their inhabitants from floods. Rather, the elevated house seems to be a cultural artifact that can be seen across Southeast Asia, perhaps a holdover from a much earlier period when early inhabitants of the region lived in trees.

Recent archaeological findings set the beginning of the Bronze Age in Southeast Asia at from 2000 to 1000 B.C.E. By around the beginning of the Common Era, there were large human settlements in north-western Thailand and northern Vietnam, marked by manmade earthworks and moats—indications of some type of political organization. The Khmer people probably developed as an independent civilization at about the same time. They seem to have acquired metalworking skills independently, and to have gradually created a distinct social order. At this early stage of the development of Khmer civilization, many elements of Indian culture were incorporated through contact with Indian traders active on the southern coast of Cambodia. The process of Indianization took place over a very long period of time, gradually influencing Khmer life. The introduction of Indian-style tools and implements such as harnesses, plows, and oxcarts are indications of this influence, as are, in the cultural sphere, the adoption of writing, numbers, and certain literature and artistic motifs. The great Indian epic, the *Ramayana* (*Ream Ker* in Cambodian) was to have a tremendous influence on Cambodian culture, becoming such an integral part of Cambodian life that villagers today believe it is their own cre-

The Mekong River, which nurtured the Angkor civilizations.

ation. The Khmer rulers adopted Hindu beliefs, especially the worship of Vishnu and Shiva, which they adapted to native customs and beliefs. Later, Mahayana Buddhism was transmitted to Cambodia, bringing with it such popular figures as the bodhisattva Avalokiteshvara, and still later, in the thirteenth century, Theravada Buddhism was introduced, becoming the religion of most Cambodians today.

The first native state to emerge in Cambodia existed in an area of the southern Mekong delta and was called "Funan" by the Chinese in their chronicles. Funan seems to have been established some time in the first century of the Common Era, primarily as a trading state. Creation and foundation myths have come down to us, including the story of a *naga* king, a water deity, who created the world by drinking

up the waters of a flood. Another story finds the origins of the Funan kingdom in the marriage of the Indian Brahmin Kaundinya to a *naga* princess. Funan was the recipient of Indian influences over a long span of time. Elements of Indian material culture as well as social, political, and religious influences were absorbed and adapted, and a native state with Indian structures was established. The rulers of Funan used many elements of Indian culture primarily to establish and bolster their authority. They brought Indians of the Brahmin caste to their courts and included them in their retinues, for example, but Indian culture did not penetrate deeply into the life of the people.

The extent of Funan's trade activities is testified to by the rich trove of objects that have been unearthed at Oc Eo, a major

Houses on stilts along the Sen River.

A bronze Buddha from Oc Eo (sixth century).

port of Funan located on the coast of the Gulf of Siam in the modern Vietnamese province of Long Xuyen. Among the artifacts are trade goods from India and the Roman Empire to the West, and from China to the east.

At its peak, Funan exerted territorial control and cultural influence over neighboring states, one of which was called Chenla by the Chinese, or Kambuja in the native language. Chenla was centered at the area on both sides of the Mekong River in southern Laos, near the ruins of Wat Phu. In about 550, it gained its independence from Funan. In the seventh century it grew in power, eventually absorbing Funan, and around 613 established its capital, Isanapura, in the Sen River region at Sambor Prei Kuk, Kompong Thom Province. Later Chenla split into northern and southern territories, and by 715, it had broken up into several small kingdoms.

THE EMERGENCE OF THE ANGKOR KINGDOM

The founder of the Angkor kingdom, Jayavarman II (r. 802–34) seems to have spent some time as a captive in the area near or in Java, returning to his homeland in the second half of the ninth century. He took up residence on the plains near the northwest shore of Tonle Sap, the Great Lake, in the vicinity of Roluos or Hariharalaya, which would be one of his future capitals. Jayavarman II vigorously engaged in military campaigns throughout Cambodia that increased his territory significantly.

He built a temple on Phnom ("mountain" or "hill") Kulen, about forty kilometers from the shores of the Great Lake, where he installed and worshiped a sacred linga representing Shiva. It was there that, in a ceremony borrowed from Hinduism, he had himself crowned "god-king," or *devaraja*, thus bolstering his political authority with religious underpinnings. It is unclear exactly how Jayavarman II instituted this idea of divine kingship, but no doubt he was already regarded with awe because of his military prowess. Relying on Hindu doctrines and also invoking native deities—Phnom Kulen had previously been regarded as the home of a Khmer god—he seems to have been able to assert his own divinity and establish a tradition of divine kingship.

The third Angkor ruler, Indravarman I (r. 877–89) expanded his territory to include almost all of modern Cambodia.

Sambor Prei Kuk, the capital of Chenla.   *Phnom Kulen (photo by Y. Ishizawa).*

Indravarman I was the first great royal builder, constructing several large temples and other buildings in the area around Roluos, which was his capital, about thirteen kilometers east of the city of Siem Reap. His first project was the Preah Ko temple complex, dedicated to the spirits of his royal ancestors. This was followed Bakong, a mountain-temple on a grand scale to house the royal linga. Indravarman also had the enormous reservoir of Indra-tataka built, with walls of earthen dikes.

Yasovarman I (r. 889–c. 910) built the first royal capital to be located in the Angkor area, Yasodharapura. Centered on the hill of Phnom Bakheng, the complex was four kilometers on each side. At the peak of the hill he built a temple to house the royal linga. This central temple complex was a symbol of Mount Meru, with galleries extending in the four directions. It was a representation, according to Hindu cosmology, of the realm of the gods. Yasovarman I also built a huge reservoir, East Baray, measuring 7 by 1.8 kilometers. Yasodharapura was only eight kilometers from the Great Lake. Many river boats traveled to it from the lakeside port of Phnom Krom, which was not only an important area for lake and river traffic and a bustling trading center of forest products but also came to

be known as the maritime gateway to the Angkor capital.

Two rulers with brief reigns followed quickly after Yasovarman I. The next great king was Jayavarman IV (r. 928–42), who built a new capital, Koh Ker, about ninety kilometers northeast of Angkor. A mountain-temple similar to that at Angkor was constructed at Koh Ker, and the capital remained there for seventeen years.

Rajendravarman II (r. 944–68) moved the capital back to Angkor, where he built the mountain-temple complex Pre Rup. War with the kingdom of Champa began about 945. The Chams were a people living in the coastal areas of central Vietnam, where they had established a trading and maritime state influenced by Indian civilization from an early period. In the year 1000, Jayavarman V (r. 968–1001) initiated the construction of the mountain-temple complex Ta Keo (uncompleted) and built a royal palace. A high-ranking Brahmin official serving under Jayavarman V built the temple of Banteay Srei, one of the most beautiful creations of Angkor art.

Later rulers of Angkor built Preah Vihear in the Dangrek Mountains north of the Thai border, and in the Angkor area Baphuon temple, the huge reservoir West Baray (eight kilometers by two kilometers),

Phnom Bakheng at Yasodharapura.

Phimai, built in about 1108.

and other works. During the reign of Jayavarman VI (r. 1080–1107), Phimai temple in northeastern Thailand and Preah Khan temple at Kompong Svay, Kompong Svay State, were built.

THE PEAK OF THE ANGKOR KINGDOM (TWELFTH-THIRTEENTH CENTURIES)

In 1113, Suryavarman II had himself crowned king by the Brahmin Devakara-pandita, a high-ranking royal advisor and tutor. Suryavarman II is the builder of that great work of world architecture, the temple of Angkor Wat. Angkor Wat is a mountain-temple with a series of three concentric galleries. Five towers connected by galleries crown the elevated central sanctuary, which is sixty-five meters high. A roofed cruciform cloister connects the second and third galleries. Angkor Wat was dedicated to Vishnu. Suryavarman II was regarded as a manifestation of Vishnu, and after his death Angkor Wat became his tomb.

During Suryavarman's reign, large temple complexes were built outside of the Angkor area as well. Beng Mealea, at the foot of the southwestern cliff of Phnom Kulen, is perhaps the most famous and is

of such a grand scale that it has been called the "Eastern Angkor Wat."

Suryavarman II was a warrior king. He led his forces as far at Vietnam (Dai Viet), fighting against the Ly dynasty. He also went on to war against Champa, with which he had previously formed an alliance, and later attacked the Mon people of the Hari-punjaya kingdom in central Thailand. By the end of his reign, he had extended the Khmer Empire from southern Laos to the Gulf of Siam, and from the border with Pagan in the west (modern Myanmar) to Champa in the east. Suryavarman II is thought to have died sometime between 1145 and 1150, and the cause of his death is unclear. In the thirty years following, there was a succession of short reigns of weak or tyrannical kings, creating a period of instability. In 1177, Cham forces invaded Cambodia, sailing up the Mekong to the Great Lake, from which they attacked Angkor and occupied it.

At this time, the next ruler, Jayavarman VII (r. 1181–c. 1220), was enmeshed in bitter fighting within Cambodia. He was about fifty years old. He won a great victory in a naval battle against the kingdom of Champa on the Great Lake, which is depicted in the relief carvings of the galleries of Bayon and Banteay Chhmar. In about 1203, Jayavarman VII conquered

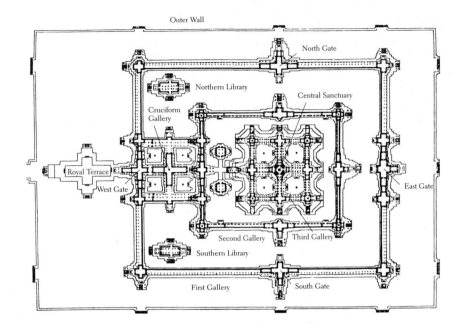

Plan of Angkor Wat.

Champa, which remained under Khmer rule until about 1220.

Jayavarman VII was a follower of Buddhism. He is said to have been a man of deep religious faith and great kindness and compassion. A stone stele inscription proclaims that "the king feels the sufferings of the people as keenly as if they were his own." He build one hundred and two "hospitals" throughout the kingdom, and one hundred twenty-one resting places for travelers along the roads (later to be called the "royal roads"). He also marshaled the peasantry to carry out engineering projects, and nearly completed a network of roads linking the entire nation. The main roads were paved with stone, so that chariots drawn by elephants could use them and also so that they would remain passable during the rainy season, when dirt roads turned to mud. The road system made it possible to deliver products, as well as tribute in the form of rice and other goods, from all over the kingdom to the capital of Angkor. A portion of the road built at this time is still in use, as a part of National Highway 5, and many stone bridges from the period still survive in Kompong Chikreng Province and other areas.

Jayavarman VII's greatest architectural achievement was the construction of the capital of Angkor Thom ("Big City"), which is laid out in a square with the Bayon temple complex in its center. Bayon is distinguished by its fifty towers with huge faces of the bodhisattva Avalokiteshvara on all four sides. A wall of red laterite stone eight meters high surrounds the city, and of its five gateways, three face north, south, and west and two face east. Each of the

A battle on the Great Lake from a relief at Bayon.

gates is topped with a four-sided tower, again with Avalokiteshvara faces on each side. The gentle smiles of the faces have come to be known as the "Khmer smile." A wooden monastery was located on an adjoining site outside the city walls.

Preah Khan and Ta Prohm temples are also located nearby, and Banteay Kdei temple just a little farther removed. There were also many small and medium-sized wooden temples in the area. Jayavarman VII also built Banteay Chhmar (located near the Thai border, in Banteay Menchen Province), on a scale equal to Angkor Wat. Many other temples were also constructed in Cambodia during his reign. Every construction effort was accompanied by large-scale engineering projects, and large numbers of local residents were conscripted as corvee labor to complete them. This resulted in regional development throughout the empire.

Jayavarman VII also restored the royal terrace at Angkor Thom City, and rebuilt the Elephants Terrace and the Terrace of the Leper King adjacent to it. He was the greatest builder of all the kings of Angkor, and with his death, the age of such enormous construction projects came to an end as well

THE DECLINE OF ANGKOR

After the death of Jayavarman VII, Khmer forces began to be pushed back from their foreign conquests. They left Champa in 1220, and in the same year they were driven from Sukhothai in central Thailand by a Siamese headman who then proceeded to crown himself king of the Sukhothai kingdom. This was the beginning of the Thai military threat to Cambodia, which would surface in later years.

The thirteenth century was a time of great change in Khmer society, as well as in Southeast Asia in general. During the reign of Jayavarman VIII (r. 1243–95) there was a strong resurgence of the Hindu faction in the Angkor court and a vigorous reaction against Buddhism, which had held sway under Jayavarman VII. In the thirteenth century, Theravada Buddhism was introduced to Cambodia, with its tradition of rigorous monasticism. A stone stele in Pali, the canonical language of Theravada Buddhism, dated 1309, commemorates the establishment of a Theravada temple. Up to that time, Angkor's government and religion had been based on the teachings of Hinduism and Mahayana Buddhism, but from the thirteenth century Theravada Buddhism replaced them as the spiritual foundation of the

The West Baray and fields in the dry season.   *Doing laundry in the Siem Reap River.*

empire. It quickly spread among the Cambodian people and became the dominant religion.

After a final stele dated 1327, Old Khmer and Sanskrit stele inscriptions disappeared, signifying the decline of the Khmer Angkor dynasty. In 1352, Thai forces from the kingdom of Ayutthaya attacked Angkor. They attacked on two more occasions and finally took the city. Historical materials aren't sufficient to provide a clear picture, but it seems that by around 1431, Angkor had been abandoned.

From the ninth to the mid-fourteenth century, the Angkor dynasty was undeniably the most powerful force in Indochina. We have an enormous amount and variety of architectural artifacts from that civilization, including temple complexes, monasteries, roads, and reservoirs, as well as such architectural decorations as pediments and lintels, dancing girls (*aspara*), female divinities (*devata*), soldiers, and other figures both in relief and fully sculpted.

When historians discuss the reasons for the glory of Angkor, they always cite its irrigation systems. The control of water made intensive rice cultivation possible. The French scholar Bernard Philippe Groslier has recently described the capital cities of Angkor as "*cité hydraulique*," or "hydropolises."

In the region surrounding Angkor Wat, the water supply system centered on the East Baray and the West Baray. The reservoirs were fed with water from the Siem Reap River, which flows even during the dry season, and from plentiful rainfall. At its peak, the maximum flow rate of the Siem Reap River is 400 cubic meters of water per second. The spacious Mount Kulen highlands also have a heavy annual rainfall (2050 millimeters), which drains into the Siem Reap and guarantees its flow even during the dry season.

The reservoirs of Angkor were not excavated but built by enclosing a large flat area with raised earthen dikes. Water collected within the dikes and was distributed by opening sluices and allowing gravity to carry the water out and down. The availability of water in these reservoirs meant that supplementary irrigation could be carried out on a regular basis, and also that water was available during periods of drought. This made multiple rice crops (probably three per year) possible, even during the dry season, which in turn supported an extremely high population density.

The wealth of the Angkor period is directly linked to this agricultural base, and a superb irrigation system is what made high agricultural production possible. It is important to remember, however,

A river of Phnom Kulen (photo by Y. Ishizawa).

that only a very limited amount of land in the Angkor area was irrigated: according to Groslier's estimates, about 70,000 hectares (700,000 square kilometers). This is not nearly enough paddy land to supply a secure source of food to the large number of laborers required for the construction of the huge temple complexes of the area.

Additional human resources in the form of large-scale corvee labor were necessary, and part of this workforce was made up of war captives and slaves.

WATER CONTROL IN ANGKOR

Put in the simplest form, Angkor's prosperity was determined by its successful control of water resources. The Angkor region has a dry tropical climate, with an average annual rainfall of about 1,500 to 2,000 millimeters. Water storage was, from ancient times, a necessity for the inhabitants of the area. It was during the Angkor period that a successful means of preventing flooding during the heavy rainfalls of the southwest monsoon and at the same time storing that water for use in the subsequent period of the dry northeast monsoon was developed. The great achievement of Angkor civilization was the difficult engineering feat of controlling the waters of the secondary rivers and the rainfall of

the annual wet season, and it was this success that supported the growth and development of Angkor.

The Angkor region is a large, fan-shaped area surrounding the Siem Reap River flowing down from Mount Kulen. Strict and careful control of reservoirs was necessary to grow three rice crops per year. In 1998, the Japan International Cooperation Agency completed a 5000:1 topographical map of the Angkor region. The map shows the existence of the East Baray, almost the same size as the West Baray, and to the east of it. Two other large reservoirs were also identified. The detailed topographical survey revealed many new historical facts. Contour lines spaced fifteen meters apart reveal the topography of the land in great detail, showing a series of earthen dikes running east to west, parallel to the walls of the reservoir.

The terrain naturally slopes down from northeast to southwest, and many small earth ridges have been built perpendicular to the slope-parallel, in other words, to the south wall of the West Baray. The wall of the West Baray could be opened to allow water to flow up to the first dike, covering the area in between with a shallow layer of water. This area could then be planted with rice, and its dike opened to release water into the next field. This, it is theorized, was the irrigation method employed in Angkor. The great kings built the reservoirs, controlled the release of water, and saw that the rice paddies were irrigated. Three months later, the rice crop was ready to harvest. Angkor Wat, rising above this hydropolis, was a symbol of an empire of water.

This cycle of rice production, carried out three times a year, was the secret to the prosperity of Angkor. According to stone inscriptions, the king regularly visited the Mebon temple in the middle of the reservoir to perform ablutions, but recent discoveries have shown that there may have been a practical use for the visits as well: a metal pipe at Mebon leading into the middle of the reservoir was used to measure the water level of the reservoir.

THE FRAGILE GLORY OF THE GOD-KING

The prosperity of Angkor was due to the intensive rice cultivation made possible by a superb irrigation system. Traces of similar irrigation systems can be detected throughout Cambodia, as well as the Sukhothai region in central Thailand, northeastern Thailand, and the Champasak region of Laos. These brilliant achievements were the fruit of the efforts of many, many laborers.

Just how were so many workers marshaled? Part of the motivation may have been religious. Since the king was regarded as a god, an incarnation of Shiva, the king of all gods, labor dedicated to the king may have been regarded as holy service. Faith in water deities and water myths were also prevalent in ancient Cambodia, from the ubiquitous *naga* to the Hindu myth of the Churning of the Ocean of Milk, depicted in so many temple reliefs. The political and military might of Angkor was always supported philosophically by Hinduism and Mahayana Buddhism, and the doctrine of the god-king was a prime tenet of these philosophical systems.

Interestingly, Angkor and the irrigation systems that supported it declined after the introduction of Theravada Buddhism in the thirteenth century. One of the main teachings of Theravada Buddhism is the abandonment of all things of this world in the single-minded pursuit of personal enlightenment. This austere monastic religion rejected, of course, the idea of the *devaraja* and the identity of the king with the Hindu god Shiva. With the adoption of Theravada Buddhism, Angkor lost the philosophical and religious pillars of that

An ancient road to an Outon-dynasty site.

Siamese forces depicted at Angkor Wat.

supported its system of government and its spiritual values. This triggered a weakening of the infrastructure of the kingdom.

A strong military force was necessary to preserve and defend the king's glory. The "royal roads" that led to every region of the realm not only made possible the delivery of goods and tribute to the royal capital but also played a useful role in quelling local rebellions. But the roads led both ways. As the kingdom of Ayutthaya arose in Siam from the early fourteenth century, the center of Thai power shifted southward to the present Chao Phraya delta. Thai military forces were able to pass through the Aranyaprathet region directly to the outskirts of Angkor, using the very royal roads the Angkor kings had built to strike at the empire's heart.

Faced with a challenge to their central belief system and the prospect of imminent foreign invasion, the people of Angkor no longer maintained the irrigation systems. The reservoirs and culverts silted up and became unusable. Without the irrigation systems, agricultural production fell precipitously—it must be remembered that the soil of the Angkor area is poor. The foundation of Angkor's prosperity was fragile indeed.

YASODHARAPURA (ANGKOR THOM) AS SEEN BY ZHOU DAGUAN

Zhou Daguan (c. 1260–c. 1346), author of *The Customs of Cambodia*, traveled to Cambodia in the party of an ambassador from China's Mongol (Yuan) dynasty. They sailed from Shizhou in February 1296 and arrived in Cambodia in July. He stayed in the royal capital of Yasodharapura for almost a year, leaving for China in June 1297. Zhou has left a detailed record of Yasodharapura in its glory, before the Siamese invaders destroyed it.

Zhou's *Customs* begins with a general introduction and continues on for forty-one entries, concluding with "The Sovereign Comes Forth." Though it certainly shows the influences of the Chinese views of non-Chinese civilizations, it is a detailed record touching on such subjects as the nature of Cambodian kingship, local industries and products, economic activities, military affairs, and the conditions of village life, making it a valuable historical source. First and foremost, the young Zhou actually visited most of the places he describes in and around the capital, with the exception of the interior of the royal palace. Second, he was able to gather

Theravada monks.   *An ancient road in Angkor Thom.*

information from the local Chinese community. Third, he lodged in the homes of Cambodians, and from them he was able to collect a wide variety of information, including oral traditions and legends.

We visit Angkor Thom and the nearby temples as ruins today, but Zhou Daguan provides a detailed account of the capital in its days of glory. "The city is twenty leagues in circumference, with five gates, each comprised of an inner and an outer gate. . . . There is a huge moat outside the city, and a large bridge over it connects it to a great highway. Fifty-four stone images of deities stand on each side of the bridge, like great stone generals. They are large and imposing." He also notes that the royal city's gates are guarded, and that they are opened in the morning and closed again at night. Upon entering the city, he says, you come first to the Bayon temple complex.

"There is a golden tower," he writes. "And close by there are more than twenty stone towers and more than one hundred chambers. A golden bridge leads to the east, and two golden lions sit one on each side of the bridge. There are eight golden Buddhas in a row below the stone chambers."

Of Angkor Wat, Zhuo writes, "There is a mountain of stone towers outside the south gate, at a distance of about one-half league. Legends say that Lou Pan built it all in one night. Lou Pan's tomb is just a bit over one league from the south gate. The whole temple complex is ten leagues in circumference, and there are several hundred stone chambers in it." He seems to have believed that Angkor Wat was a tomb, and perhaps the local Chinese called it the tomb of Lou Pan, who was an ancient legendary Chinese god of artisans.

The area around the Elephants Terrace at the front of the royal palace is now overgrown by forest, but Zhou describes it in its heyday. "The royal palace, residences, and offices all face east. . . . The roof tiles of the main building are manufactured of lead. . . . The pillars and beams are huge and carved with images of the Buddha, so that the chambers are quite grand. There are two levels of long galleries, which stretch high into the sky and are built according to a regular plan."

Zhou Daguan was impressed by the huge palace complex, shining gloriously under the burning tropical sun. But all of the tall wooden towers he saw stretching into the sky were destroyed when the Siamese forces attacked, and today not a trace remains. He tells us that the palace in which the king carried out his duties had windows with gold frames, and mas-

A Brahma bull pulling an oxcart from a relief at Bayon.

sive square pillars embedded with mirrors supported the roof. It must have been a truly marvelous sight.

The Daily Life of Cambodians in the Angkor Period

Zhuo Daguan also did some keen cultural reporting based on his observances of the Cambodian people and their customs. "Most inhabitants wear only a single piece of cloth wrapped around their waists, and men and women alike expose their breasts. They bind up their hair and are barefoot." He continues, "If any family has a beautiful daughter, she is always sent to serve in the palace. . . . Ordinary women wear no hair ornaments, combs or other decorations. They do wear gold bracelets on their arms and gold rings on their fingers." These descriptions would have applied equally well to the inhabitants of Cambodian villages until very recently.

Relief carvings of the Bayon temple complex give us a glimpse of daily village life. No doubt Zhou Daguan passed such scenes on the road—oxcarts pulled by two Brahma bulls with their characteristic humps, people riding in palanquins, and others on horseback. Certainly he must have seen the peddlers carrying their goods hanging from poles across their backs, and stopped and looked at the fruits and fish spread out in the market stalls before the shopkeepers. He may also have seen cockfights and boar fights. Cockfights are still one of the favorite entertainments of village men in Cambodia.

The markets were run by women. "All trade in this country," Zhuo writes, "is conducted by women. . . . There are no shops. The vendors spread a mat out on the ground, and each has a designated place. I have heard that though there are no shops, the vendors do pay rent to the officials for the space they use." The markets were permanent and active places of business to which villagers brought their homegrown onions, garlic chives, eggplants, watermelons, and cucumbers and spread them out on mats to sell, just as is shown in the relief carvings.

Zhuo Daguan also noted the clothes and ornaments of the women at the markets. Cambodians wove their own cloth, and, he said, "there are various grades of cloth. . . . they weave cloth in this country, and it is also imported from Siam and Champa, but Indian cloth is regarded as the finest." He was a sharp observer. Zhuo Daguan seems to have had an interest in

A bustling market outside Siem Reap.　　　　　　　　　*Making pots without a wheel.*

trade between China and Southeast Asia before he made his journey, and his record is particularly interesting because of the sections dealing with Cambodia's forest and other local products.

The reliefs at Bayon depict housing in the villages as well. Pots and hearths are set on the ground, and there is no furniture to speak of. We can see water jars, pots, and unglazed bowls and plates, as well as a few simple pieces of furniture made from palm fronds. This is true of most rural Cambodian dwellings even today.

"In ordinary homes," he writes, "there are no tables, chairs, bowls, or buckets. They do use an earthenware pot to boil rice or to prepare soup. A hearth is built by half-burying three stones in a circle. Coconut shells are used as ladles, and when they serve rice in a dish, they use an earthenware or copper platter of Chinese manufacture. They serve soup in little bowls made from leaves. These bowls are cleverly made and do not leak."
Such were the furnishings of a middle-class household.

Zhou reports that the most important of all annual observances was the Cambodian New Year, which was celebrated in April. Foreign ambassadors and dignitaries were invited for the occasion,

fireworks were lit, and the populace celebrated noisily for two weeks.

CAMBODIA AFTER THE FALL OF ANGKOR

Though the ruler of Angkor was absolute, claiming to be identical to Shiva and thus divine, there was no established system of succession. Very rarely was power handed over smoothly, and in most cases there was a bitter struggle. Blood brothers, brothers by different mothers, and brothers by marriage all made succession claims in Angkor's history, and of course each candidate for succession also had a faction that surrounded and supported him. A king acceded to the throne in a religious coronation ceremony in which the Brahmins played a crucial role. Since there were no accepted laws of succession, over the centuries there were numberless plots, betrayals, and conflicts surrounding the matter.

These battles over succession seem to have continued after the fall of Angkor, but there is little historical material from that period and details are scarce. The only source is the *Chronology of the Cambodian Court*, compiled much later. The earliest extant example of that work is a fragment presented to the King of Siam

Scenes of daily life in Angkor from a relief at Bayon.

in 1796. There are also printed versions from the nineteenth and early twentieth centuries.

The capital of Angkor Thom was abandoned, but Angkor Wat continued to be used, converted from a temple to Vishnu to a Buddhist temple. In the latter part of the fifteenth century, the image of Vishnu in the central sanctuary was replaced with a four-meter Buddha image. As a Buddhist temple, it attracted the faithful of the area, and even as far away as India it was known for its great beauty. From the latter half of the twelfth century, it became a widely known Buddhist holy site and visitors from all over Southeast Asia came to worship there, often leaving inscriptions.

There are fourteen examples of Japanese inscriptions at Angkor recording visits to Angkor Wat. The best known is

that of Fujiwara no Ason Morimoto Ukondayu Kazufusa. Traveling thousands of leagues across the seas, he arrived at Angkor and visited the temple on New Year's Day, 1632. In about twelve lines of writing, he records having donated four Buddha images. Ukondayu's father Morimoto Gidayu was a senior retainer of Kato Kiyomasa, and he had fought in the Japanese invasion of the Korean Peninsula. Ukondayu's voyage took place in the early years of the Tokugawa shogunate, established by Tokugawa Ieyasu in 1603. At this time, the Japanese government was officially sanctioning intercourse with other nations, and there was a brief flurry of overseas travel. Communities of Overseas Japanese sprung up in the countries of Southeast Asia. The ruler of Cambodia in this period was Chey Chetta II (r. 1619–27),

An Outon-style temple.　　　　　*Buddha images at Preah Peang.*

and the capital was in Oudong, some forty kilometers north of Phnom Penh.

The inscriptions of Japanese visitors are concentrated in the area of the cruciform cloister in the center of the temple complex. This was known as Preah Peang, or "The Thousand Buddhas," and in the past more than two thousand Buddha images, large and small, were installed there. Even today it is a holy site constantly visited by local worshipers. Angkor Wat has changed its robes to those of Theravada Buddhism, but it continues to exist as a religious center.

The Japanese who visited here in the seventeenth century seem to have believed that Angkor Wat was Jetavana, an important Buddhist site in India during the Buddha's lifetime. A "Map of Jetavana," now in the Shokokan Museum, Mito City, and said to have been brought back to Japan by one Shimano Kenryo (perhaps a pseudonym, place of birth unknown), an interpreter from Nagasaki, is clearly a map of Angkor Wat, recording with considerable accuracy its orientation, the moat, and the galleries.

Ukondayu returned to Japan in 1632, and moved with his father back to his father's place of birth, Yamazaki in Kyoto, where he died in 1674.

BANTEAY CHHMAR, THE GREAT MONASTERY HIDDEN IN THE FOREST

André Malraux (1901–76), later to become France's Minister of Culture, described in his novel *La Voie Royale* (1930) a "Royal Road, desolate and slowly disintegrating," but still running like a maze crisscrossing the dense jungles of Cambodia. In ancient times, the northwest of Cambodia was a dense tropical forest, and the road, sometimes a raised earthen path and sometimes paved with stone, ran through the forest in all directions. In his novel Malraux describes "the buried temples, the stone Buddhas covered in moss, and one Buddha with a tree frog sitting on its shoulder" in the ruined city in the jungle. This royal road, however, was not fiction; it really exists. All of the royal roads led to the capital of Angkor. The roads leading to the northwest cross the Dangrek Mountains and reach northeastern Thailand. The large-scale temple complex Banteay Chhmar is located along the royal road, in an area that was an important center of activity in northwest Cambodia in days gone by. Banteay Chhmar is some one hundred fifty kilometers northwest of Angkor, and

The site of Jetavana, in north India.

only twenty-two kilometers from the Thai border. Built by Jayavarman VII in the thirteenth century, it is a flat (rather than a mountain) Buddhist temple complex of approximately the same size as Preah Kahn. A moat 65 meters wide runs the 3 kilometers of its circumference. A reservoir 1.6 kilometers by 750 meters is located on the east side of the temple, and eight shrines with towers are located nearby the large complex of buildings.

Banteay Chhmar was first surveyed by the École Français d'Extrême Orient in 1910, and its main features are well known, but no attempts have been made to preserve it. Banteay Chhmar displays the same architectural and decorative style as Bayon at Angkor. The gateways at the north, south, east, and west entrances are decorated with scenes from the famous Hindu narrative of the Churning the Ocean of Milk, with *ashuras* and *devas* tugging back and forth on the body of a *naga*. The cruciform terrace at the main (east) entrance and the twenty-five-meter gate are decorated on all four sides with faces Buddhist figures. There are ten stone inscriptions

here. The interior layout has a complex but orderly layout of towers in the architectural style of a monastery. The galleries have the same style of bas-relief friezes as seen at Bayon, realistically depicting the battle with the Chams on the Great Lake and their rout by the Khmer forces. A unique feature of this gallery is its beautiful bas-relief image of a thousand-armed Avalokiteshvara. In the past, between 150,000 and 200,000 people resided in this region, and as the carefully maintained reservoir indicates, it possessed an extensive irrigation network. According to the French scholar Georges Groslier, some 20,000 laborers or villagers worked daily for from twenty-seven to thirty years to complete this temple-city complex.

REST STATIONS AND HOSPITALS

Interestingly, one of the 121 rest houses built by Jayavarman VII is located within the east gate of Banteay Chhmar. Today about 50 of these rest houses have been

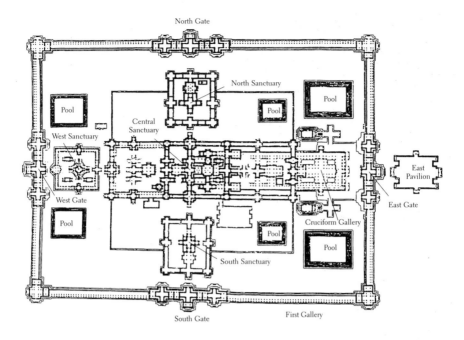

North Gate

North Sanctuary

Central
Sanctuary

West Sanctuary

Pool

Pool

Pool

Pool

West Gate

Pool

East
Pavilion

East Gate

Cruciform Gallery

Pool

Pool

South Sanctuary

South Gate

First Gallery

Plan of Banteay Chhmar.

identified. Called dharmashala (houses of the Buddhist Law) in stone inscriptions, they were designed to offer officials and villagers traveling along the road a place to rest. They were also called "hearth houses," and the Chinese visitor Zhou Daguan also notes their existence during his residence in Angkor: "There are places to rest on the main highways, similar to our Chinese post-stations." The construction of the rest houses was a manifestation of the king's compassionate bodhisattva practice toward the villagers, and they were built along all the main roads. They were directly linked to the regional administration of the period. Inscriptions also record the construction of 102 "hospitals" at important regional centers, of which 33 have been identified to date.

I visited the region in 1961 and 1968

to carry out scholarly surveys, including taking rubbings of inscriptions and sketching diagrams of the reliefs. I then visited Banteay Chhmar again after three decades, in 1996. We left the Siem Reap airport by helicopter on the afternoon of November 8, and landed at our destination about forty minutes later. The first thing to strike one when viewing the site from the air is the rampant forest growth. Looking more closely, the surrounding moat and part of the galleries is visible. The site of the reservoir was dry, and the Mebon temple sat in its center. There was a village nearby, surrounded by rice paddies.

Fallen stones and trees and thick undergrowth growing from beneath blocked the approach leading into the complex. We entered from a break in the surrounding walls and began our survey, taking photo-

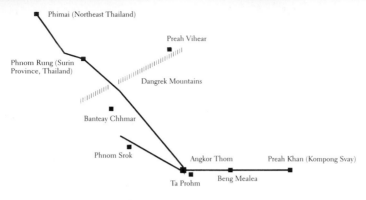

The road system of ancient Cambodia.

graphs and establishing our position. The tower gates, sanctuaries, and central sanctuary had almost completely collapsed, and fallen stones lay on top of each other. It was a very dispiriting sight. With map in hand, we walked the site identifying the locations of the buildings, climbing over the fallen stones and weaving our way through the forest growth. It had been left untouched for the last thirty years, with no restoration activities.

The central sanctuary, once thirty-five meters high, has completely collapsed into a huge pile of stone. Thirty years ago, several of the tall towers and sanctuaries were standing, if precariously, but now huge trees covered them all. As we faced this massive pile of fallen stones brought down by the unstoppable forces of nature, the full extent of the destruction was manifest. In addition, the faces of *devatas* had been cut out of the reliefs. Clearly, the site was being looted.

The Cambodian Ministry of Culture and Fine Arts and authorities of Banteay Mechen Province must work together to find the best way to restore and preserve these large complexes of completely collapsed ruins.

Today there are four overgrown sites equal to Angkor Wat in importance at which no preservation or restoration activi-

ties are going on: the royal capital at the beginning of the seventh century, Sambor Prei Kuk (Kompong Thom Province); Koh Ker, a major city for seventeen years in the early tenth century (Siem Reap Province); Beng Mealea, also known as "the eastern Angkor Wat" (Siem Reap Province); and Preah Kahn of Kompong Svay, along the royal road in central Cambodia (Kompong Thom Province). All of these sites are waiting for much-needed assistance.

We have continued to monitor these four sites and Banteay Chhmar based on satellite photographs, and in the on-site survey in 1996 we acquired data indicating the advanced degree of their destruction. It is clear that as yet undiscovered elements of Khmer civilization exist at these five sites. We have reported on the dire need to preserve and restore these five sites and urged the authorities to take action.

THE CLIFF TEMPLE PREAH VIHEAR AND THE HILL TEMPLE PHNOM RUN

Preah Vihear, meaning "sacred temple," is built atop a cliff of the Dangrek Mountains, some 600 meters in altitude. A long stone walkway 850 meters in length

The cliffs of the Dangrek Mountains, with forests below.

stretches from the approach to the temple up to the main sanctuary. Though located just inside Cambodia, it is actually easier to reach Preah Vihear from the Thai side of the border. It is about three hours from the little Thai town of Sisaket, which is about 110 kilometers from Kantharalak.

Inscriptions at the temple record that Yasovarman I initiated construction of this temple at the beginning of the tenth century. At the time, it was a wooden structure. During the reign of Rajendravarman, stone and wooden sanctuaries were added, and during the reign of Jayavarman V a main sanctuary and two "libraries" were built. In 1026, Suryavarman I (r. 1010–50) added to the growing complex with monk's quarters and living quarters. The surviving structures date from this period. Many inscriptions were also made at that time and wooden buildings were also constructed. Later, during the reign of Suryavarman II, the high official Divakarapandita carried out further additions at the behest of the king. Preah Vihear was a holy site from early times, and kings of every generation visited it.

The architecture and architectural decoration of Preah Vihear belongs to the styles of the late *khleang* to Baphuon, and the pediments and lintels are striking. Rahu (an *ashura* who was thought to

devour the sun and moon during eclipses), Lakshmi, and four-headed Brahmas are depicted. The temple is dedicated to Shiva, Lord of the Gods.

Architecturally speaking, its unique feature is the way in which galleries surround the main sanctuary. This development triggered a shift in building technology, and is thought to be an antecedent to the galleries of Angkor Wat. The central sanctuary represents Mount Meru. The most distinctive feature of the temple, of course, is its natural setting and the rising approach to the main building from the west. As in the case of Angkor Wat, the approach from the north leads to the main entrance. From the temple one can see the shimmering surface of the Great Lake.

As the royal road runs from the city of Angkor, passing over the Dangrek Mountains into Thailand, the first temple one encounters is Phnom Rung, built in the tenth century on a hill about 170 meters high. The entrance to the temple faces east, and a stone-paved causeway 300 meters in length leads up to it, following the contours of the land. After climbing a flight of steps, one arrives at a cruciform terrace. Another flight of steep steps leads up to the main building, which is enclosed by rectangular galleries (88 meters by 66 meters). The main sanctuary rises up

Shiva from the central sanctuary at Phnom Rung.

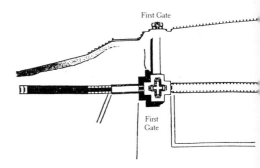

First Gate

First Gate

inside the enclosure and still retains some of its past glory. Kings of each successive reign added to the complex throughout the eleventh and twelfth centuries. There are no dates on the stone inscriptions, but the name of Suryavarman II, who built Angkor Wat, appears in them. Phnom Rung is located along the royal road about halfway between Angkor and Phimai.

Descending the hill on which Phnom Rung is built, one encounters a large reservoir still filled with water. About 3 kilometers down the road that runs past the west side of the reservoir, a small stone building stands in the middle of a banana plantation, one of the 121 hospitals built near the royal road. The faces of Avaloki-teshvara that decorated it on four sides have crumbled and fallen without a trace, but the general form of the small stone building can still be made out.

Villages dot the broad plain that extends out from here, and traveling to the west one arrives at Prasat Muang Tam. Enclosed by an 800-meter wall, it has gates on the north, south, east, and west. Inside the enclosure are four small L-shaped ponds, and farther into the center is an inner enclosure surrounded by small galleries. Much of the large central sanctuary of the level, five-sanctuary plan still stands. The other four sanctuaries are small and

arranged in a unique pattern, one on either side of the large sanctuary and two behind it. There are also two "libraries." The five stone inscriptions carry dates from 959 to the thirteenth century, and the temple is linked to Suryavarman II and his royal house. The temple was dedicated to Shiva, and mention is also made of the ancestral king Rajendravarman. A large reservoir 3 kilometers by 2 kilometers is adjacent to the temple site.

The royal road continues on to Phimai, often called "the Thai Angkor Wat" because of its refined and dignified appearance. The ogival central tower is a majestic reminder of ancient grandeur. It rises shimmering above the surrounding sugar-palm planta-tions in a setting very similar to those of Cambodia temples in ancient times. The temple is approached from the south, and the outer enclosure is a square 1.6 kilome-ters on a side. The walls are pink sandstone and enclose galleries running around the enclosure. The central tower stands in the middle of the enclosure. A typical Angkor-period temple, in a level, cruciform plan, Phimai is believed to have been built around 1108. Interestingly, a statue of

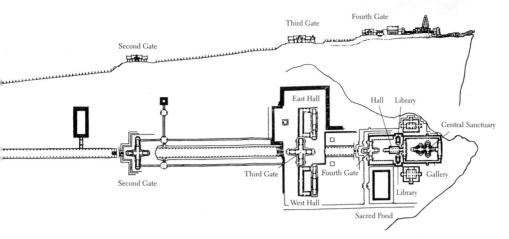

Elevation (above) and plan (below) of Preah Vihear.

Jayavarman VII was discovered in this temple. In early times, Phimai was the center of Angkor's northwest territories (present-day northeast Thailand), and no doubt the king's statue was installed and worshiped here. It is in the Angkor Wat architectural style, and the Shiva and Vishnu provide the main themes of the architectural decoration of the ogival central tower, the pediments, and the lintels, though there are also depictions of Buddha seated on a *naga*. In Thai art history, Phimai is categorized as belonging to the Lopburi Period (eleventh to thirteen centuries). The main construction materials are pink sandstone and laterite.

THE NORTHWEST BORDER OF ANGKOR: SUKHOTHAI

The royal road proceeds north from Phimai, then turns north-northwest into the middle reaches of the Chao Phraya River and arrives at Sukhothai. The first native Thai kingdom, Sukhothai flourished from the thirteenth through fifteenth centuries, and was the cradle of Thai culture. Sukhothai was a regional capital built by the Angkor kingdom on the northwest border of its territory. In the mid-thirteenth century, two Siamese chieftains drove out the Khmer governor of the area and established the kingdom of Sukhothai. During the reign of the third Sukhothai ruler, Ramakamheng (r. 1279–98), Sukhothai's territory expanded as far as Louangphraban in Laos to the north and the Malay Peninsula to the south. In the same period, Theravada Buddhism was introduced to Sukhothai, becoming the source of the ideals of government as well as the inspiration for architectural and artistic styles.

The religious architecture of the ruins of the ancient city of Sukhothai incorporates cultural elements from various sources—Sri Lanka, from which Theravada Buddhism was transmitted to Thailand; neighboring Burma; the Mon people of southern Thailand; and the Khmers to the east—and combines them to create a distinctively Thai artistic style. The lotus-bud finial at the top of a pagoda (*chedi*), as seen in the central sanctuary of Wat

Prasat Muang Tam.

A Sukhothai Buddha image.

Mahathat, became a distinguishing feature of the Sukhothai architectural style. In sculpture, a distinctive style of Sukhothai Buddha image also developed. The famous Walking Buddha of Si Sachanaray is a good example, with its spiral-curled hair, "wisdom protuberance," and tuft of white hair between the eyebrows, curling to the right (from which the Buddha emits a beam of white light), and characteristic expression.

San Tha Pha Daeng is the oldest surviving Khmer building at Sukhothai, and was built during the reign of Suryavarman II. Its superstructure has collapsed, and the pediments and lintels are gone, leaving only the infrastructure. Hindu deities in the Angkor Wat style were discovered within it. Siamese chieftains under the suzerainty of the Angkor kingdom ruled Sukhothai, and a Khmer princess was sent in marriage to the local ruler.

Si Sachanaray was a secondary capital some sixty-five kilometers north of Sukhothai. Two groups of ruins stand in an open area on the north bank of the winding Yom River. The region on the east side is called Chaliang, and it is the location of what is thought to be the northernmost of the 121 rest houses built by Jayavarman VII in the early thirteenth. This is Wat Chao Chang. To the west are the ruins of a capital city, surrounded by a laterite wall

almost five meters high. The walled enclosure is square and about four kilometers in circumference, surrounded by a moat ten meters wide. Inside the enclosure are the remains of nine structures, the largest of which is the temple Wat Chang Lon, which has thirty-nine elephants carved into its base.

To the east of Wat Chang Lon stand the many tower-sanctuaries of Wat Chedy Chet Yot, which display a wide variety of artistic influences, including Khmer, Mon, Burmese, and Sri Lankan, in addition to the distinctive Sukhothai style. This was also the center for Sangkhalok pottery, thought to have developed during the Sukhothai period through the incorporation of techniques from Yuan-dynasty China. To date, 145 kiln sites have been identified. Both underglaze iron painting and celadon were produced at Sangkhalok kilns, and their production was an important trade item with the kingdom of Ayutthaya to the south, which was linked to Sukhothai by the Yom River. The production of the Sangkhalok kilns ended in the seventeenth century.

Wat Mahathat at Sukhothai.

LOPBURI AND AYUTTHAYA: THE REMAINS OF KHMER TEMPLES IN THE LOWER REACHES OF THE CHAO PHRAYA RIVER

Suryavarman I of Angkor expanded his rule to Lavo (Lopburi) in the middle reaches of the Chao Phraya River, driving out the Mon people who lived there. At the time, this was the westernmost outpost of the Angkor kingdom, which was attempting to extend its domination into northeastern Thailand.

Several small and medium-sized stone temples in the Khmer style were built in the Lopburi region. On two occasions, 1115 and 1155, Lopburi sent independent trib-

ute missions to China, in an attempt to shake off Angkor's rule, but by the reign of Jayavarman VII, the area seems to have come once again under Angkor's sway. Among the remains noteworthy for their architecture and art are the sanctuary of Wat Pra Phrang Samyot; the pyramidal Wat Nakon Kosa, now collapsed; and Wat Mahathat, which has been repaired and rebuilt on several occasions. From the Buddha images that have been discovered at these sites, it is evident that a workshop of artisans producing art in the Khmer style was active in this area. Eventually the architecture and art of Lopburi had a strong influence on Ayutthaya, and, merging with the Sukhothai style, gave birth to the Outon style.

Stone inscriptions in Ancient Khmer have been unearthed from Lopburi. Wat

Wat Chang Lon at Si Sachanaray.

Wandering monks from Wat Mahathat.

Pra Phrang Samyot, characterized by three connected towers, stands in the middle of the city of Lopburi. One can still sense the original majesty of the seven-story ogival sanctuary in the Khmer style. The pediments, lintels, and other decorative elements have been lost. The sanctuary is made mostly of sandstone, with some brickwork as well.

Wat Mahathat displays the influence of past Khmer styles combined with Sukhothai-style architectural features. It was built from the end of the fourteenth to the early thirteenth century. Parts of it also show characteristics of the Lopburi style, making it valuable for verifying the transition from the Sukhothai to the Lopburi style. The tower sanctuary is in the Khmer style, and Sukhothai-style elements can be detected in the four corners of the tower, the lintels, the stucco carving of the base, the decorative motifs, and the sculptures.

The Sukhothai kingdom was absorbed by the Ayutthaya kingdom, with its capital in Ayutthaya, in central Thailand on the lower reaches of the Chao Phraya River. Ayutthaya was designated the capital in 1351 by Ramathibodhi I, the founder of the kingdom, and remained so until 1767. There are more than five hundred temples and pagodas in the city, and it was a flourishing center of the arts of Theravada Buddhism, but Burmese forces attacked and completely destroyed it in 1767, and all the glory of the dynasty was reduced to rubble. Viewing the ruins today, however, it is still possible to catch a glimpse of the proud magnificence of the capital in its heyday.

Wat Mahathat was built in the early Ayutthaya period, blending the Lopburi and Sukhothai styles. The three stupas of Wat Si Sanpet were built in the fifteenth century, when the Sukhothai style with its bell-shaped stupas became dominant. From the mid-seventeenth century, the Pra Phrang style, incorporating Khmer-style, tall ogival sanctuaries was created. Ayutthaya reached its peak in the years from 1732 to 1762, and many Buddhist temples were built at that time. Due to its location, Ayutthaya was able to effect a consolidation of various cultural elements from Lopburi, Khmer, Sukhothai, Burmese, and Mon civilization, combining them all with the Thai people's special talent for assimilation. In architecture, this is evidenced in the Pra Phrang style, and in sculpture in the Outon school, a blending of Lopburi, Sukhothai, and Shrivijaya styles.

The royal road dating from the Angkor period survives in Thailand as far as Sukhothai. It runs through northeastern Thailand, passing through Phnom Run and Phimai. Another branch passes over the Dangrek Mountains into the Aranyaprathet region,

The central sanctuary at Wat Mahathat.

reaching the lower reaches of the Chao Phraya River and the Lopburi area. From the fourteenth through the fifteenth centuries, Ayutthaya forces in the tens of thousands used this road through Aranyaprathet to attack Angkor. From that time, role of leading civilization of the region passed from Angkor to other dynasties and kingdoms.

THE ROYAL ROAD TO THE EAST: BENG MEALEA AND PREAH KAHN

Another royal road ran from Angkor to the south and east. Actually, it was a system of roads, one of which is the modern Highway 5.

Beng Mealea is about forty kilometers to the east of Angkor, though it takes four hours to get there because there is no direct route. It is slightly smaller than Angkor Wat. The moat is 45 meters wide and the circumference of the temple complex is 4.2 kilometers. It was built about twenty years before Angkor, from the end of the eleventh through the beginning of the tenth century, by several kings, including Suryavarman II and his predecessors.

The layout, design, towers, and galleries of Beng Mealea are almost identical in style to those of Angkor Wat, though on a smaller scale. Architecturally speaking, techniques predating those employed at Angkor Wat are in evidence. Round whorls of scrolling vines (*karakusa*), interlocking rings, and images of devatas distinguish the bas-reliefs of the galleries and the architectural decorations, which have not been studied to date. The history, composition, and structure of this site are only now becoming clear, as comparative studies of Angkor Wat and Beng Mealea are carried out. The site, including the reservoir (1.5 kilometers by 600 meters) and the entire temple and town complex (4.2 kilometers in circumference occupies a total of 108 hectares.

Beng Mealea was the largest regional center in the Angkor vicinity. It developed, like Angkor, as a city-temple "hydropolis" with an advanced irrigation system, and it was an important stop on the ancient road leading to the east. There is evidence of large population concentrations in this area, including communities that provided workers for the construction of Angkor.

I conducted a survey of the site in 1961; it was then off limits from 1970 to 1996. When I arrived for a second survey in 1997, I recorded and photographed the dramatic destruction that rampant growth of trees and underbrush had wrought. I also surveyed the looting that had taken place and reported it to UNESCO.

Preah Kahn temple, in Kompong Svay, lies on the royal road as it leads to Champa, about 105 kilometers southeast of Angkor. It is part of Kompong Thom Province, though it is located deep in the mountains, 120 kilometers distant from Kompong Thom City. In the past, the royal road passed through Beng Mealea and reached Preah Kahn, and the route was well traveled. Today, portions of the road, though in bad condition, are still used to travel between the local villages.

The temple is surrounded by a large moat 4.8 kilometers on a side, and adjacent to the moat is a square reservoir 2.8 kilometers on a side. It was built during the reign of Jayavarman VII at the beginning of the thirteenth century, and the central sanctuary has Buddha faces on all four sides. In the past, a *dharmasala*, or rest house, was located near the outer walls.

This seems to have been a regional city before the time of Jayavarman VII, and the name of Suryavarman I has been discovered on stone inscriptions here. The grounds of the temple are spacious, and though today forest has overtaken them, in the past there were wooden houses, temples, and monks' quarters. An earthen dike surrounds the inner side of the moat, and a double row of galleries circles the central sanctuary. The temple is laid out in a cruciform shape, oriented to the east. The galleries around the central sanctuary are about 48 meters on a side, and are open on all sides. The central sanctuary has collapsed into a pile of rubble. What appear to be the foundations of several temples and monks' quarters are nearby, but they are buried in the forest growth. The entire complex is larger than Angkor Thom, and must have been magnificent in its time.

THE RIVER ROUTE TO WAT PHU

Sailing up the Mekong River, past the cities of Kratie and Stung Treng, one arrives as the Khone Falls on the Laotian side of the border. After disembarking and traveling overland, one sets sail again above the falls, in the area that was once the kingdom of Champasak.

The decline of the ancient kingdom of Funan, in southern Cambodia, seems to have begun with the unlawful accession to the throne of Radravarman (r. 514–c. 550), which fanned internal divisions. After Radravarman's death, however, remnants of the government survived to send tribute missions to China.

The Champasak region, at the convergence of the Mekong and Mun rivers (now

Wat Phu and Mount Lingaparvata.   *The main temple at Wat Phu.*

in southern Laos), was the cradle of the newly risen Khmer (or Chenla, as they are known in Chinese sources) forces that attacked and defeated Funan. Ancient sites from the fifth century and stele inscriptions have been discovered in the vicinity of Wat Phu.

Khmer (Chenla) was previously a vassal state of Funan, but it gradually grew more powerful and prosperous. Information about Chenla is recorded in the *Sui Shu* (edited by Wei Zheng and others during the Tang dynasty and completed in 636) and other Chinese sources. There are no Khmer or Sanskrit equivalents to the Chinese term "Chenla," which is a Chinese transliteration of the name of the kingdom's ruler Chetrasena Mahendravarman.

A stone inscription, probably from the end of the fifth century, reads, "The supremely blessed Sri Lingaparvata, is worshiped here," indicating that the area around Wat Phu was already regarded as sacred at that time. The *Sui Shu* also states, "Near the city is a mountain called Lingaparvata, with a sanctuary on its peak. It is constantly guarded by five thousand soldiers." The present Wat Phu is built on the mountain slope and makes good use of the natural site. There is a main sanctuary and attached buildings, all from the same period. Subsequent generations of Khmer kings,

beginning with Yasovarman I, visited Wat Phu, which is built from sandstone and laterite and has two large ponds at its foot.

THE ROAD TO THE CHAMPA KINGDOM

The kingdom of Champa existed from the end of the second century to the seventeenth century in the area of what is now central and southern coastal Vietnam. It adopted Indian-style government and religion. The Champa kingdom flourished as a corridor for trade. In the late fourth century, Badhravarman I built a temple to Vishnu at the holy central Vietnamese site of Mi Son. In later centuries, Champa was afflicted externally by military pressure from the Chinese in the north and attacks by the newly arisen Vietnamese kingdom in northern Vietnam, and internally by many swift changes of rule, and it gradually retreated southward. Champa was also attacked from the west by Angkor. Champa was actually a loose federation of trading ports along the coast, each governed by a local ruler. The kingdom flourished as a trade zone linking India, Southeast Asia, and China. A single king did not rule over a central government; rather, there were many kings,

The Champa Museum at Da Nang.

joined in a kind of federation. When one of them was especially strong and powerful, the others followed him, but trade was carried out nearly autonomously at the various centers of the empire.

In this long history of federation and disintegration, a separate and relatively stable dynasty existed in Phan Rang (in those days known as Panduranga) in the south. Several sites with architectural remains from this period survive. Mi Son and Tra Kieu, south of Da Nang, have remains of Shivaite Hindu temples, and there are Buddhist remains at Dong Duong. At Binh Dinh (Vijaya in the Cham period) there are the famous examples of *kalan*-style architecture, the gold, silver, and copper towers, and the Thap Man sculptures. In Nha Trang (Kauthara in the Cham period) there is the Po Nagar sanctuary and in Phan Rang there are the Po Klong Garai, Hoa Lai, and Po Rome sanctuaries. These Champa centers were all lost as the Vietnamese pressed the Chams southward, and Champa almost disappeared, but coastal centers to which Cham villages had fled across the Southeast Asian mainland continued to be active. There is a Cham Museum at Da Nang, and it is possible to view the changes of Champa's history there.

Champa produced important art and architecture from the tenth through the eleventh centuries. Perhaps most distinctive is the architectural style called the *kalan* style, with a multilayered, pyramidal roof placed on top a square tower. The use of *makara* demon masks and vegetal motifs such as twining vines also distinguish this style of architecture. Records state that when Po Nagar was restored in 1050, after having been burned down several times, ambassadors from Khmer, China, Thailand, and Pagan visited the temple and paid their respects. The existing structure, however, dates from the thirteenth century.

This region developed as a trading center from about the second and third centuries, and it was near here, in the region of Nha Trang, that the Vo Canh inscription, the oldest stone inscription in Southeast Asia (circa the third century) was discovered. In the eighth century, the Javanese attacked from the sea and burned Po Nagar to the ground. It flourished afterward as the center of southern Champa, until it was conquered in 1653 by the powerful Southern Vietnamese Nguyen clan. *Kalan*-style sanctuaries from several different periods survive.

Panduranga (Phan Rang) was a political center of south Champa from the eighth century. The hilltop sanctuary facing the sea is a Hindu temple in the distinctive *kalan* style. Enduring pressure from Vietnam and attacks from Cambodia, Panduranga

The "gold tower" atop a small hill outside Qui Nong.

Po Klong Garai at Phan Rang.

survived into the mid-seventeenth century as an outpost of the Champa kingdom. Even today, many Chams live in this region.

The Po Klong Garai sanctuary is a Cham sanctuary built by Jaya Simhavarman III in the early fourteenth century. It is a typical example of the *kalan* style, with a five-tiered pyramidal tower set on a square brick base. It is, however, of the later *kalan* style, built as the kingdom of Champa was declining. There are no traces of the bas-relief carving on the outer walls or architectural decoration, and the false doors on three sides are in the form of pediments. These sanctuaries reflect the declining fortunes of the Champa kingdom.

A Meeting of Fiction and Nonfiction: André Malraux's *La Voie Royale*

When Henri Mouhot first introduced Angkor Wat to the West in 1861, he wrote, "The population of this nation, which has been engaged in endless strife with its neighbors, has been decimated. I estimate that at present it stands at less than one million." The first French director-general of Cambodia, J. Moula, gave the nation's population in January 1874 as 945,974, of

which 746,424 were Cambodian by descent. These figures did not include the populations of the provinces of Battaban, Siem Reap (until 1907 a part of Thailand), or Strung Treng (then a part of Laos). If these provinces had been included, the population would have probably been about 1.1 million. By any measure, Cambodia was a depleted nation.

With the establishment of the French protectorate in 1863, Cambodia lost its independence but gained safety from threats by its neighbors, and it entered a period of peace.

As we have seen, ancient Cambodia was traversed by a network of royal roads. One story of the rediscovery of those roads began in December 1923. The hero of the novel was one Claude Veanek, a graduate of the Paris Institute of Oriental Studies. Arriving in Saigon with his new wife, Claude sails up the Mekong River, traveling past Phnom Penh to Siem Reap, the city nearest the ruins of Angkor. There he meets a famous archaeologist of the École Français d'Extrême Orient. A party of four—Veanek, the archaeologist, his assistant and close friend, and a guide—set out on a journey deep into the jungles of Cambodia in search of hidden ancient ruins.

About thirty-five kilometers to the

Banteay Srei.

northeast of Angkor Wat they come upon an archeological site of great beauty. It lies at the base of Phnom Kulen, a source of quarry stone, on the upper reaches of the Siem Reap Rive that flows through Angkor. The small temple with a level layout is called Banteay Srei, or "The Women's Citadel." It is 95 meters by 110 meters in size and was built in 967 as a funerary temple by the Brahmin Yajunyabharaha.

Banteay Srei was built of pink sandstone, and the walls, lintels, and pediments of its three sanctuaries, set on a foundation about one meter high in the innermost of three enclosures, are covered with wonderful reliefs depicting Hindu myths. Among all of the delicate and beautiful sculptures and reliefs, the *devatas* holding blossoms and guardian *dravapalas* at the four corners of the north sanctuary are particularly outstanding. The figures stand about one meter tall and possess an indescribable sense of movement and beauty that stirs the heart and excites the senses.

The hero of the novel, with his superior aesthetic sense, is quick to apprehend the importance of the lovely sculptures. In reality, Banteay Srei had been discovered in 1914 and two years later a detailed survey had been published, identifying it as of the first rank artistically. Our hero and the rest of his party spent three days

removing seven blocks of stone from the site, after which they packed them up and carried them back to Siem Reap. From there they boarded a ship and set sail across the Great Lake and back down the Mekong, only to be apprehended by a government official at Phnom Penh. They were confined to their hotel on charges of destroying and looting an archeological site, and finally sentenced by the French representative in Saigon to a suspended sentence of one year's imprisonment, plus the return of the stolen art.

The hero of this novel is none other than Malraux himself, who is said to have stolen a relief of a devata holding a flower and the pediment surrounding the figure. Malraux's devata is a sensuous figure, but at the same time pure and artlessly charming, with lovely robes and ornaments. Over the years it has come to be known as the Mona Lisa of Asia.

Malraux used the experiences of his explorations of the ruins of Cambodia as the material for his novel *La Voie Royale*, published in 1930. Claude Vaneak is Malraux, and bears a very close resemblance to his creator. The journey from Marseilles to Siem Reap as described in the novel matches perfectly with Malraux's own journey with his bride, Clara. The esteemed professor of the French Academy

A devata holding a blossom at Banteay Srei.

in the novel is modeled after the previous director of the École Français d'Extrême Orient, Louis Finot, and his assistant and the young Cambodian guide who accompanied them to Banteay Srei also correspond to real people.

The plot of the novel revolves around the search for the ancient royal roads of Cambodia that have remained hidden in its tropical jungles for more than a thousand years, and the eventual discovery of the a beautiful temple along the road. *La Voie Royale* is not simply a tale of heroic adventure but the story of a search for eternal beauty and enduring value. Certainly we can say that the royal roads of ancient Angkor and what they represent played a role in forming the character of Malraux, an advocate of a dynamic humanism.

The great sites of Angkor are a symbol of the unity of the Cambodian people today and a great cultural legacy of which they are, deservedly, very proud.

PHOTOGRAPHER'S AFTERWORD:
ANGKOR'S LONG SILENCE
AND A NEW DAWN
By Hitoshi Tamura

During the early 1970s, the three nations of Indochina were wracked by war. At the time, journalists and photographers covering Indochina used to get together in the bars of Roppongi, in central Tokyo, and I was among them. It was an exciting time for photojournalism, and the photographers who risked heir lives to capture that special moment on the battlefield were the heroes of our profession. Most of those gathered in the Roppongi nightspots in those days were freelancers, but people from the major papers, the magazines, and the publishing companies were also regular members of the scene. The group ranged from *Life Magazine* staff photographers to kids just out of college, but we all treated each other as equals when we argued, which we did with great regularity. What did we argue about? Mostly about the war going on in Indochina, but we also talked, when discussing the history of Cambodia and Vietnam, about the ancient empires of Angkor and Champa. Whenever you went to Roppongi, you heard something new about what was going on in Indochina, and I got many ideas for stories to cover from those late-night discussions.

From about that time I was based in Bangkok, and I often traveled into Cambodia, Laos, and Vietnam. For a time, I was taking pictures of the war. But that was never my main interest. I focused on the history and culture of the countries, the background against which the war was being played out. Throughout that whole period, I had an image in my mind that I could never forget: those great ruins of an ancient kingdom, Angkor Wat and Angkor Thom, slumbering in the midst of the battle.

Because of the war, I only really had access to the area around the capitals and a few other sites. In Vietnam, I was once stranded for several days when fighting suddenly broke out on National Highway One, leading from Huey to Saigon. There were times when I was photographing in some small rural town only to find myself surrounded by Vietcong forces, and completely isolated. Even though I wasn't covering the war, there was no place that wasn't far from a battlefield. I was able to photograph Cham ruins in the middle of towns or along the roads at that time, but it was impossible to get anywhere near sites in the mountains, such as Mi Son—which, by the way, was bombed and partially destroyed because it was a Vietcong stronghold. In Cambodia, the Khmer Rouge occupied almost all of the Angkor ruins, including Angkor Wat itself.

I still have three negatives of Angkor Wat I shot in December 1973. I took them with a 300-millimeter lens, on the front lines of the government forces, about a kilometer from Angkor Wat. From that distance, I could barely make out the towers of Angkor Wat with my naked eye. The government forces were firing rockets on Angkor Wat. Knowing what was going on, I assumed that the temple complex had suffered considerable damage. I was also very worried about another photographer, Taizo Ichinose, who had traveled to a Khmer Rouge "liberated zone" near Angkor just a few weeks ago. At the time, the Khmer Rouge lines were only twenty kilometers outside Phnom Penh, and rockets were hitting the capital, which could have fallen any day. In April 1975, the Khmer Rouge toppled the Lon Nol government and the People's Democratic Republic of Kampuchea was established. Later, from the time Pol Pot came to power, a period of tyranny and genocide began, and Cambodia was completely closed to the outside world. For a long time after the wars in Vietnam and Laos had come to an end, it was still impossible to photograph there. My dream of photographing Angkor-related sites seemed doomed to failure.

I decided to shift my focus from Indochina to India. Over its long history, India has produced a great and highly varied culture that has been a major influence, and even a source, of the cultures of Southeast Asia, China, and Japan, and I had always wanted to photograph there. Learning that many of the cultural features of Southeast Asia that I had been interested in, such as the temple ruins, classical theater, and dance of the nations of Southeast Asia, had roots in India, I threw myself into photographing India with great enthusiasm. I traveled there every year, and lived there more than half

of each year. After long years of working in India, my understanding of the Hinduism and Buddhism that had been transmitted from there to Southeast Asia changed, and at the same time I was motivated to return to Southeast Asia. I wanted first of all to photograph the remains of Angkor civilization. The glimpse of Angkor Wat I caught in the midst of battle remained engraved on my mind. The harder it was to actually see and photograph Angkor, the more fascinated with it I became.

It only became possible to photograph in Southeast Asia in the later 1980s. But even then, the local governments tightly controlled all travel, specifying the hotels foreigners must stay in, the vehicles they must drive, and the guides they must use, as well as the areas they might visit. All of this went for a very high price, in spite of the fact that you were not free to photograph what you wished. I have always had a hard time working with a fixed schedule and a deadline; to me it has always seemed that the strength of being a freelancer is that one can pursue your subject without such restrictions until you are satisfied with your work. After several years of working under the governments' rules, most of Vietnam and Laos became open to travel. At last my work became enjoyable. But there were still many areas in northwest Cambodia, where Pol Pot's forces held out to the bitter end, that I could not enter because they had been land-mined, or because the area was still not secure.

I first planned this book quite a while ago. I had photographed in open areas, such as Thailand, Laos, Vietnam, and the area around Angkor Wat several times. It was the first time, however, I worked in most of central and southern Cambodia. Security had been a problem, making these areas difficult to get to, of course, but in addition there was a lack of information about this area, and almost no photographs. Nothing had changed since thirty years ago, when I first traveled to Southeast Asia. In those days you could learn little about Southeast Asia in Japan; you really had to just go there and find out for yourself, starting from square one. In photographing in Cambodia for this book, the first step was to travel to a village or town near the site I wanted to photograph, and then find someone there who knew the site. Often getting there was the major challenge. There are no reliable roads leading to sites that have not been restored. Roads appearing on maps suddenly stop, or aren't passable. On the other hand, there were many moments that made it all worth it: when I encountered one of the royal roads that are the theme of this book, or when I came across scenes of daily life that were unchanged from the ancient times when they had been sculpted into the bas-reliefs on temple walls.

My aim as a photographer in this book is to put Angkor Wat and the temples in its immediate vicinity, which have been the subject of many books, into its larger context, showing the many other temples, capital cities, sacred places, and other sites that appear in the histories of the Angkor kingdom. In addition, by photographing sites along the system of roads that led from the capital to the empire's regional cities, I wanted to impart a sense of the vast scale of Angkor's civilization, and, in some small part, contribute to an understanding of the empire as a whole entity. I included ruins of the Champa and Ayutthaya empires, which had engaged in battle with Angkor time and time again, to allow the peoples who had become part of the Angkor empire their time on stage and in an attempt to capture the full span of Angkor from its beginnings, its rise and fall, its prosperity and decline.

I have tried to introduce as many as possible of the sites that could not be photographed until now because of the wars in the region. But there are still ruins sleeping in the jungles of ancient Angkor, some reputed to be even larger than Angkor Wat. Unfortunately, for security reasons, it was still impossible to visit these sites. I can only wait for the day when we will have free access. Cambodia is only now awaking from its long nightmare of war and destruction.

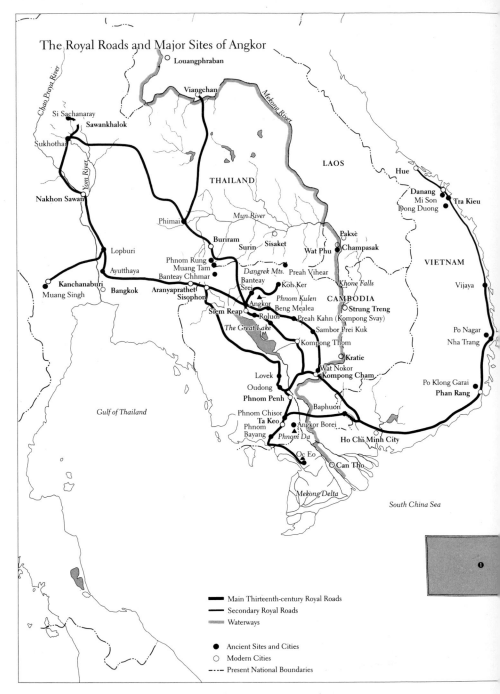

The Royal Roads and Major Sites of Angkor